Hartman Rector, Jr.

No More Strangers

VOLUME 2

Now therefore ye are no more strangers and foreigners, but fellowcitizens with the saints, and of the household of God;

And are built upon the foundation of the apostles and prophets, Jesus Christ himself being the chief corner stone. (Ephesians 2:19-20.)

No More Strangers

VOLUME 2

HARTMAN AND CONNIE RECTOR

BOOKCRAFT INC.
SALT LAKE CITY, UTAH
1973

Library of Congress Catalog Card Number: 72-175136

2nd Printing, 1973

LITHOGRAPHED IN U.S.A.

PUBLISHERS PRESS
SALT LAKE CITY, UTAH

CONTENTS

PREFACE

The testimony of the Saints is the strength of the Church. Peter's admonition, "Be ready always to give an answer to every man that asketh you a reason of the hope that is in you. . . ." (1 Peter 3:15), is a plain injunction to us to testify of the truth which we have received through the gospel of Jesus Christ.

Testimony implies conversion. To testify means to bear witness to that which you now *know* to be true. For example, one may say, "I know that Jesus is the Christ." Now, this is fine, but *how* do you know? What was the experience that gave you this knowledge? *That* is what strengthens and builds your brethren. The Master said to Peter: "When thou art converted, strengthen thy brethren." (Luke 22:32.) That must have come as a shock to Peter. He had already borne testimony in bold words that his friend Jesus was the Christ: "Thou art the Christ, the Son of the living God." (Matthew 16:16.)

But Peter had a problem which Jesus discerned. It severely limited his ability to perform the service he was selected to perform—that of "strengthening the brethren." He could not strengthen his brethren until he was converted himself and until he had a testimony that the doctrine, including the resurrection, was a reality.

What was Peter's problem? He had a very common weakness. He could not bring himself to tell the truth about his association with the Master when he thought the disclosure would put his life in jeopardy. He had not yet gained the strength that conversion brings. Therefore he could not provide the strength that others needed, for he needed to be strengthened himself. Mere belief or supposition that a doctrine is true is not sufficient to support a man when a severe trial comes, because belief alone is not strong enough. Knowledge or testimony is required.

Of course, when Peter was converted he no longer feared for his mortal life. He was able to face his persecutors and bear a powerful testimony of his association with Jesus. Peter became a tower of strength from whom all could gain strength. He could then strengthen his brethren, which he did.

The Prophet Joseph Smith taught that the ancient saints were able to endure all their afflictions and persecutions and to take joyfully the spoiling of their goods because they *knew* (not merely believed) that they had a more enduring substance or, as Paul says, ". . . we have a building of God, an house not made with hands, eternal in the heavens." (2 Corinthians 5:1.)

The key to gaining a testimony or knowledge is sacrifice, or paying the price. Conversion costs something. (For one thing, it costs us our sins, and they are often dear to us.) Everything in this life has a price.

In the Sixth Lecture on Faith, the Prophet Joseph Smith teaches the principle in such plain terms that it cannot be misunderstood:

> For a man to lay down his all, his character and reputation, his honor, and applause, his good name among men, his houses, his lands, his brothers and sisters, his wife and children, and even his own life also—counting all things but filth and dross for the excellency of the knowledge of Jesus Christ—requires more than mere belief or supposition that he is doing the will of God; but actual knowledge, realizing that, when these sufferings are ended, he will enter into eternal rest, and be a partaker of the glory of God. . . .
>
> Let us here observe, that a religion that does not require the sacrifice of all things never has power sufficient to produce the faith necessary unto life and salvation; for, from the first existence of man, the faith necessary unto the enjoyment of life and salvation never could be obtained without the sacrifice of all earthly things. It was through this sacrifice, and this only, that God has ordained that men should enjoy eternal life; and it is through the medium of the sacrifice of all earthly things that men do actually know that they are doing the things that are well pleasing in the sight of God. . . .
>
> It is vain for persons to fancy to themselves that they are heirs with those, or can be heirs with them, who have offered their all in sacrifice, and by this means obtain faith in God and favor with him so as to obtain eternal life, unless they, in like manner, offer unto him

the same sacrifice, and through that offering obtain the knowledge that they are accepted of him."

It was in offering sacrifices that Abel, the first martyr, obtained knowledge that he was accepted of God. And from the days of righteous Abel to the present time, the knowledge that men have that they are accepted in the sight of God is obtained by offering sacrifice. . . .

Those, then, who make the sacrifice, will have the testimony that their course is pleasing in the sight of God. . . .

"But those who have not made this sacrifice to God do not know that the course which they pursue is well pleasing in his sight; for whatever may be their belief or their opinion, it is a matter of doubt and uncertainty in their mind; and where doubt and uncertainty are[,] there faith is not, nor can it be. For doubt and faith do not exist in the same person at the same time; so that persons whose minds are under doubts and fears cannot have unshaken confidence; and where unshaken confidence is not[,] there faith is weak; and where faith is weak the persons will not be able to contend against all the opposition, tribulations, and afflictions which they will have to encounter in order to be heirs of God, and joint heirs with Christ Jesus; and they will grow weary in their minds, and the adversary will have power over them and destroy them.

This is in harmony with Moroni's words in Ether 12:6: ". . . Wherefore, dispute not because ye see not, for ye receive no witness until *after* the trial of your faith." It accords also with the Master's statement in John 7:16-17: "My doctrine is not mine, but his that sent me. If any man will *do* his will, he shall *know* of the doctrine, whether it be of God, or whether I speak of myself." The Savior didn't say that you will know these things are true, and then you will do them. What he did say was that if you will do these things, you will know they are true.

Surely, sacrifice does bring forth the blessings of heaven— the blessings of knowledge of God (which is testimony) and which, coupled with honesty, brings about the change in a man's life which is known as conversion. Peter's statement, "Seeing then that all these things shall be dissolved, what manner of persons ought ye to be . . ." indicates that when the truth comes we must do something about it. Conversion has to do with the putting off of the "natural man," which is selfish, conceited, impatient, intemperate, disobedient and rebellious, and becoming "a saint through the atonement of Christ the Lord." This means becoming even "as a child, submissive, meek, humble, patient, full of love, willing to submit to all things which the Lord seeth fit to inflict upon him, even as a child doth submit to his father." (Mosiah 3:19.)

This change leads inevitably to service to our fellow man or works of righteousness which, after all, is the only way we can serve God. King Benjamin's explanation is still valid: "And behold, I tell you these things that ye may learn wisdom; that ye may learn that when ye are in the service of your fellow beings ye are only in the service of your God." (Mosiah 2:17.)

Then, testimony, a witness borne to the heart by the Holy Ghost, having to do with a knowledge of God, is associated with sacrifice, and when coupled with the power of faith and endurance in righteousness, produces conversion. This testimony we are commanded to bear before the Church and the world, that all may see the marvelous light of Christ that shines in the Saints and receive courage and strength to move forward in confidence that what others have received through obedience they too can receive.

This volume is intended to do precisely this. Herein we present seventeen modern conversion stories of people who are still living and breathing and striving to live the gospel every day. Their stories are in a sense their testimony and can provide the encouragement and strength necessary for others to break traditions, change habits and lifestyles, and follow the Master in this day and time as well as in generations past.

We are grateful to all the contributors for their willingness and wholehearted cooperation in permitting their stories to be published, and we join with them in expressing the hope that the book will be the means of building faith and conviction in all who read it.

We accept full responsibility for the compilation of this book. It is our own contribution and is in no way endorsed by the Church. Specifically, should any of the accounts be found to contain error, the Church and its leaders are completely absolved from responsibility for such error.

HARTMAN AND CONNIE RECTOR

CURTIS E. LEDBETTER

SOMEONE CARED ENOUGH

Do you appreciate the knowledge and understanding your Church membership brings? Do you find joy in knowing for certain the answers to such questions as:

What is my Heavenly Father like?

Is the Holy Spirit a real personage?

Did I live before I was born on earth?

Can I have a family relationship with my loved ones after death?

Many fine people outside the Church don't know for sure the answers to such questions. The Ledbetters didn't, even though Curtis Ledbetter was a Methodist minister serving as an air force chaplain. They might have still been in that situation. But today they all enjoy the joys and blessings of membership in The Church of Jesus Christ of Latter-day Saints — because someone cared enough.

This suggests an important if somewhat obvious question for us all: Is someone a Latter-day Saint, and growing in his relationship to our Heavenly Father, because of me?

The Ledbetter story is presented in three parts:

> *I The Neighbor: Johann Dobson Griffith*
> *II The Chaplain's Wife: Virginia R. Ledbetter*
> *III The Chaplain: Curtis E. Ledbetter*

1   The Neighbor

My family were stationed with the air force in San Antonio, Texas, my husband being an instructor at the Air Force Officers Training School at Lackland Air Force Base. He was also the bishop of San Antonio Second Ward. We lived in a new subdivision on the north side of town. There had been a new vacant house next door to us for several months after we moved in. In the summer of 1963 Chaplain (Major) Curtis E. Ledbetter and family moved into that house. My first contact with them was as an interested neighbor trying to help them feel welcome.

Virginia was easy to get acquainted with because she is so friendly and outgoing. My husband and I had a new baby three months old and the Ledbetters were expecting their baby in October, so we had a lot to talk about. After Virginia's baby arrived there were some occasions when I would tend her children. It was after one of these evenings that I mentioned to her what a short time ago it was when our babies had been with our Heavenly Father. I was surprised to discover that she did not have an understanding of our pre-earth life with our Father in heaven. It was at that time that the realization came to me that I had precious truths I *must* share with my dear friend. The problem was how to approach a minister's wife, who was active and dedicated in her own church, to teach her the gospel.

I am not a scriptural scholar, even though I've been taught the gospel all my life by my wonderful parents, George and Lillian Dobson. I knew I could not quote chapter and verse to back up or prove the things I knew were true. I had a great fear because of my inadequacy, but I also had a firm testimony and a strong desire to introduce the joys of the gospel to Virginia. Days would go by and I would worry and pray about it, yet I would put off actually telling her of the restored church. Then, very suddenly, a ward member died, and I had the feeling that that could be *me* tomorrow. I must not delay any longer.

Our family all knew how I felt, and now our son Lonnell made a suggestion. He said, "Why don't you write her a letter?" This seemed to me an inspired answer. Virginia could read the letter in complete privacy. She wouldn't have to feel defensive or give any kind of an immediate answer. Also, we wouldn't be interrupted by a child or a phone call. And best of all, I wouldn't embarrass her with the tears that so often come when I bear my testimony.

I fasted and prayed and then wrote the letter. We chose Elder LeGrand Richards' book, *A Marvelous Work and a Wonder*, to send with it. The letter and book were delivered to Virginia, but it was some time before there was any mention of her receiving it or any comment made about it. Those were very anxious weeks. Our entire family was concerned, and the Ledbetter family was frequently mentioned in our prayers.

When we had lived in Vacaville, California, I had sung Mickey Hart's song "The Heavens Were Opened" with our ward Relief Society. It had touched me greatly, and knowing of Virginia's love for music I wrote to my mother and asked her to send me the music for the song. The song tells of Joseph Smith's first vision. I asked Virginia if she would sing it for a ward council meeting we were having at our home. The stake mission presidency was making a presentation to the ward officers, and we felt that this song would be most appropriate.

When Virginia sang the song, it was apparent to all assembled that she had been touched by its message. After this, Virginia started to read the book I had sent her. She was eager to learn and spent hours studying, and on many days we had long discussions. As Virginia raised questions, my good husband would help me look for or tell me where to find the answers. Even our children learned a great deal, as I did, as we studied the scriptures together.

This experience taught me that we need not fear to share our testimonies, for we are never alone in those circumstances. We are then doing God's work, and he will guide and direct us in it. The Holy Ghost will add his witness to any to whom we testify if they will pray and sincerely seek to know the truth.

It was thrilling to bear my testimony to Virginia that I know Jesus Christ is our Lord and Savior and that he stands at the head of our Church. It was thrilling to witness to her that Joseph Smith was the human instrument through whom the gospel was restored in modern times, that he was indeed a great prophet, and that a prophet leads our Church today. It was thrilling to have played a small part in the conversion of such a fine family as the Ledbetters. And it was a great joy to be with them in the holy temple and see them sealed together as a family for time and eternity.

II   The Chaplain's Wife

For the first time in my husband's career as a Methodist minister serving as a Protestant chaplain in the air force, we chose to buy a home in preference to living in base quarters. At previous assignments in California, England, Massachusetts, and Morocco, Curtis had worked with families, and I felt that my place was by his side working with the Sunday School, Choir, Protestant Women of the Chapel, and Protestant Youth of the Chapel. But at Lackland Air Force Base Curtis would be working with the basic trainees. At last our two sons and I would have an opportunity to be active in a Methodist Church.

First we located the Methodist Church we wished to attend. Then in Thunderbird Hills, the first subdivision in which we house-hunted, I spotted "our house," asked to see it, and then told the salesman there was no need to look further. This "magnetic" house just happened to be adjacent to the home of the Robert Melvin Griffith family. "Mel," at that time, just happened to be the bishop of San Antonio Second Ward. We felt a special rapport with the Griffiths from the time we met them.

Johann Griffith soon became a very close friend. I adored her for being such a thoughtful neighbor. I appreciated the beautiful spirit of love in her home. We thoroughly enjoyed tending our brand new babies together, doing Cub Scout work, studying about health foods, and just talking together. Of course we went our separate ways several times each week to participate in our own church activities. We often discussed those activities (I once helped her plan a Relief Society luncheon), but we never discussed theology. Still I knew Johann was the most spiritual woman I had ever known. So dear and sweet, she personified an angel, to my thinking.

One morning during the first week of December, by my front door I found a letter from Johann and a copy of Elder LeGrand Richards' *A Marvelous Work and a Wonder.* Johann had been prompted to write the letter after one of her friends had died unexpectedly. As she grieved over the sudden loss of her friend, she reflected about her own life. In her letter she told me that she never wanted to say or do anything that would adversely affect our friendship, but that she didn't want to meet Heavenly Father without having told me that there is a prophet living on the earth today and that the true Church of Jesus Christ has been restored. Johann bore her testimony and told me a few more of her beliefs as a member of The Church of Jesus Christ of Latter-day Saints. I remember one belief which stood out luminously. She said that a man and woman and their children could be sealed together for time and eternity in a temple of the Lord. Every Christian has hope that he will be with his loved ones in heaven, but Johann wrote with a certitude that left no room for doubt. Could it be? My heart was "strangely warmed," and I remember thinking that the sensation must have been similar to what John Wesley, the founder of Methodism, had experienced when he uttered that expression. I decided that I would read the book, as she requested.

Busy, busy December! I was attending rehearsals for two cantatas (one in my own Methodist Church; one at Lackland) and helping with the Methodist Youth pageant, in addition to planning a special Christmas for my relatives. It was only our second Texas Christmas since Curtis entered the chaplaincy. (A true Texan inserts "Texas" whenever possible!) I just didn't have time to read the book! However, I did have time to feel guilty about not having read it. Johann was so hospitable to our relatives that I began to be embarrassed to see her. I made a resolution that when the New Year came I was definitely going to read enough of that book to make a few reasonably intelligent remarks about it so that she would know that I had finally complied with her request.

January came, but one morning, before I had time to commence reading, Johann showed me a sheet of music. She told me that she had first heard the song when the family were stationed in California, that she had written for the title and had had her mother in Farmington, Utah, send her the music from Salt Lake City. She had tears in her eyes as she told me it was about something very special to her. She asked me to play and sing it for her. It obviously meant a lot to Johann, so I asked her to let me take it and practice it so that I could give it my best, rather than sightread it at the time of the performance. To be honest, I thought how much simpler it would be to play and sing a song than to "get through a book" when I had a new baby. It was an opportunity to ease my conscience, because it would surely compensate, I rationalized.

How could I know that a musical composition would play such a prominent role in my life? The lovely song was Mickey Hart's "The Heavens Were Opened." The lyrics tell of a young boy named Joseph Smith who went to a grove and prayed for knowledge about which church to join. It tells of a power that tried to destroy him. Then gloriously it tells about a visitation from God the Father and his Son Jesus the Christ. Did that really happen? Could that be true? I played the song over and over; it practically haunted me. As I sang, my heart beat faster and tears would come to my eyes. I wanted to know more about Joseph Smith. Obvious solution: read the book.

I began reading the book and found it really was about a "marvelous work and a wonder." So intrigued was I that I could hardly lay the book aside. The information thrilled me, and right away I felt that it was true. The more I read, the stronger I felt about it. It was so wonderful! It was so terrible! I was frightened. I was a Methodist through and through, and I had no desire to be anything else. Besides, it wasn't expedient for me, a Methodist minister's wife, to be seriously interested in another denomination (that's what I considered the Church to be at that time)! To think of joining would be ridiculous! I decided to dismiss the thought.

It wasn't that easy. I couldn't dismiss ideas which had already penetrated so deeply. So concerned was I that I asked Curtis to read the book and "explain away" the information. It was making me uncomfortable. In a way, I just didn't want it to be true. Well, he was engrossed in a special project at the base, and in addition was taking two courses at St. Mary's University. Also, he had assumed some of the duties of the pastor of the church I attended; the pastor was incapacitated while recuperating from cataract surgery. Curtis just didn't have the time or the inclination to read the book. He assured me that there are worthwhile beliefs in every denomination—that denomination did not make any major difference. "It is your own personal relationship with God that really matters," he said.

"My own personal relationship with God." I repeated it again. For the first time in my life I was actually examining my relationship with Heavenly Father. I had been born to wonderful parents who always set a Christian example. They were active Methodists, and their parents had been active Methodists. As a child and youth, I had attended Sunday School, Morning Worship, Methodist Youth Fellowship, and Evening Worship every Sunday; in fact, the family had even attended services whenever we were vacationing away from home. I had been to Methodist Camp four summers, and the summer after my senior year of high school, at a special service atop beautiful Mt. Wesley in Kerrville, Texas, I had dedicated myself to full-time Christian service. I had attended a Methodist university, Southwestern University, and immediately made plans to choose for my marriage partner a young man who belonged to the Life Service-Ministerial Association. In time I had been blessed to marry the choicest of the group. I had taught school to help put Curtis through graduate school, Perkins School of Theology at Southern Methodist University, and we also had worked together to serve his student pastorate. In his civilian ministry and the chaplaincy we had been "a team" working with Sunday School, Youth Fellowship, Choir, and the many other facets of full-time service. I had been fortunate never to experience tragedy, and by inclination I looked at life through "rose-colored glasses," so I had never had to take the time to develop depth in my religious convictions. Although I had been gifted with a quick mind, sharp enough to graduate with honors, it would be a gross overstatement to say I was intellectual. I simply endeavored to follow the footsteps of Jesus.

Naturally, I often had questions arise in my mind. If only I could interpret the scriptures more wisely or if only I could pray with more direct communication, I would think, then I would have the answers to these questions. Although I truly wanted to be spiritual and truly wanted to know more about God, it never once crossed my mind, even fleetingly, that I might be able to find out more in another church. Candidly, I thought that the answers simply weren't available to ordinary folk. Yet in just the one book *A Marvelous Work and a Wonder* I had been exposed to more truth than I could shake off. I realized with utter dismay that I wasn't at all satisfied with my own personal relationship with God.

I wanted to know more. Daily for the next three months I studied, prayed, worried, and asked Johann questions. I had a testimony of the gospel—but what was I going to do with it? Curtis now jokingly refers to that period as the "Chicken Noodle Soup Days" because I would study until I heard his little car buzz into the driveway, and then I'd hustle into the kitchen to put on the soup for supper. One day Johann told me that I had made a better Mormon of her. When she saw my puzzled expression, she inquired, "Didn't you know I have to study every night to be prepared for your multitudinous questions?" I guess I had thought she was just a walking, talking Mormon encyclopedia!

Those of you in the mission field are aware that the "Mormon Grapevine" is a very effective mode of communication. There wasn't a missionary in the area who hadn't heard about the Methodist chaplain and his "problem." Yes, I had become a problem to him—so much so that he had become uglier and uglier about the whole situation. He said that he didn't want Johann or any other Mormon on our property and he didn't want me to go to her house. What could we do? Thank you, Alexander Graham Bell.

Then, surprisingly, one evening Curtis agreed to go with me to a musical program at the ward chapel. Afterwards in the foyer, a darling missionary, female type, went up to Curtis, batted her long eyelashes, and asked unbelievingly, "Is it really true that you won't allow a Mormon missionary in your home?"

Well, the following Tuesday Sister Lois Richardson of Bountiful, Utah, and her companion Sister Patricia Perry of Mapleton, Utah, presented the first lesson. (I still tease Curtis about that, and he still insists that he was genuinely interested to hear what they would say. Now, really!) Curtis was hospitable to them, and I was so grateful. Never once did he try to confuse them theologically. Conversely, he was impressed with their faith and testimonies. I have forgotten the point of discussion, but I haven't forgotten Sister Perry's simple declaration when asked how she knew a certain thing was true. She said: "I can't explain it by the methods you said they used in your graduate school, Brother Ledbetter, but I know it's true because the Prophet of the Lord said it is true." Moving. Moving, yes—but Curtis wasn't ready to be moved.

I was enthralled with the lessons. At the conclusion, a decision was in order, but I longed to be spared from it. Oh yes, I knew very well how damaging my joining the Church would be to Curtis's career. I had enjoyed being an "asset" to Curtis; I didn't want to be a "liability." We had often reminisced about our meeting and how fortunate we were to have found each other. Everything was changing. Even my own parents said it was heartless of me to treat Curtis so cruelly. The minister of the Methodist Church in which I had been so active was actually rude to me. The whole ordeal at times seemed unreal. I remember thinking, "This can't be happening to Curtis and me!" It was.

The following piercing remark was made to me on several occasions: "If you *really* love Curtis, you won't do this to him." That really hurt. I kept thinking of how tempting it would be to drop my intentions—if the stakes weren't so high. It isn't difficult for a sweetheart to compromise or adjust—when the matter is not of ultimate, eternal importance. This time the problem related to our salvation. Yes, *our* salvation. Love Curtis? Oh, yes, I loved Curtis! Ever in my mind was what Johann had written: "You can be sealed together forever in a temple of the Lord."

Deep down, I knew it was Curtis, precious, energetic, dedicated Curtis, that our Heavenly Father wanted in his kingdom. I honestly felt that if Curtis would let down the barrier and study for himself he would recognize the truth. But how could a man who had respect and admiration from his congregation and his colleagues, an ample income with excellent retirement benefits, and a highly regarded profession which he loved—how could such a man let down a barrier which would cause him to immediately lose all of those things? I didn't know that answer, but I did know what I had to do, and I prayed for courage to carry it through. I found solace in these words of William George Jordan:

> The man who has a certain religious belief and fears to discuss it, lest it may be proved wrong, is not loyal to his belief; he has but a coward's faithfulness to his prejudices. If he were a lover of truth, he would be willing at any moment to surrender his belief for a higher, better, and truer faith.

I knew I had found a higher, better, and truer faith.

Curtis finally gave his permission for me to be baptized and even attended the baptismal service, July 11, 1964. It was a climax to the most soul-searching experiences of my life. Curtis subsequently gave his permission for our children to go to the LDS Sunday School. He still wasn't convinced that there was enough difference to really matter. He figured that the LDS Sunday School would probably be as satisfactory as the General Protestant Sunday School the boys had attended at previous bases. This naturally meant that the children and I went one way, and Curtis went another. The more I attended meetings and studied, the more my testimony grew — and the more estranged Curtis and I became. The more excited I became the more apparently disenchanted he became. He no longer wanted to hear anything about it. Period. I thought he was stubborn not to study, and he thought I was presumptuous to join before he was ready to study. My days were filled with hopes for a unified family, and my nights became crying sessions.

Curtis wasn't the only one disappointed in me. My dear parents just couldn't understand. Their response was not one of anger or of criticism of me. Daddy, loved and respected by all who know him, asked earnestly, "Virginia, where did we go wrong?" I've tried to convince him that his example and teachings made me receptive to the gospel in its fulness when I heard it. Presently Daddy is the treasurer of the Alvin Methodist Church, where he served on the Board of Stewards and Mother served as Communion Stewardess for decades. I pray that someday they will share the great happiness that I have in my knowledge of the restored Church of Jesus Christ.

The answer to my longing to interest Curtis in some LDS activity came with Education Week, January, 1965. After much coaxing, he agreed to go. Although at the time he commented only about Dr. Richard O. Cowan's tremendous appeal as a teacher, he later told me that the memory of Brother Cowan's beautiful testimony stayed in his mind and was influential in his conversion.

Then Curtis received orders reassigning him to the Air Force Academy, near Colorado Springs. From a career point of view this was literally a dream come true, and he was elated. I was overjoyed because my joining the LDS Church hadn't prevented his being selected for the choice assignment, and he was over-joyed at the wonderful opportunity to get me out of the clutches of the Mormons! (How could he know that Heavenly Father had more "Griffith-type" Mormons at the Academy? The Batemans, Gunnells, and Watsons were precisely the saints that the Ledbetters needed!)

We arrived at the Academy the first day of March, 1965. Striving for harmony in our home, I promised Curtis that I would be active in the Protestant program. I was discouraged many times. It was hard to understand that for the same type of partici-pation for which I had previously received accolades I was then receiving derision. . . . But the Academy is a part of Curtis's story.

What a cherished gift is Johann's letter! So many wonderful things have happened since then! Surely I am a member of The Church of Jesus Christ of Latter-day Saints because someone *cared enough*. What a great blessing it was on August 8, 1966, to go to the Salt Lake Temple to be sealed for time and eternity and to have our precious children, Lynn, Lennon, and Lynda sealed to us. Previously the word *Lamanite* wasn't even in my vocabulary, and now we have a choice Lamanite son, Jerry S.

Curtis, in our home for the fourth year. He truly loves the Lord and His Church, and we truly love him. Then on November 10, 1970, our little Lyndal Lane arrived. We call her our "LDS Bonus" because it was revealed to us that she was waiting to come to our family. (Formerly we had no knowledge of the premortal existence.)

It thrills me to know that the President of the Church is a true prophet of God through whom Jesus Christ directs his people. I am especially grateful to have the priesthood—that great gift of power given to man by God to act in his name and in his behalf in righteousness—in my home. I have an inner peace, having answers to my lifelong questions, and sometimes I am so happy that my eyes fill with tears just from gratitude that I could find these answers while still in this mortal life.

I sincerely love Heavenly Father and Jesus Christ, and I pray that I will order my life so that I may be worthy to receive exaltation in the celestial kingdom. I humbly bear testimony of the divinity of The Church of Jesus Christ of Latter-day Saints, and I do so in the name of our Savior Jesus Christ. Amen.

III   The Chaplain

As Virginia says, we are Latter-day Saints because someone cared. Actually, many people cared. Still it wasn't easy. There were moments of tears, heartache, and frustration. Those moments led to a time of deep, soul-searching inquiry and, ultimately, a rich joy.

While serving in the United States Air Force, I had observed several Latter-day Saints at different activities. In doing so, I had become very impressed by their spirituality, moral character, and family unity. Often I had wondered what it was about The Church of Jesus Christ of Latter-day Saints that produced people of such quality. Therefore, when the opportunity was afforded me to discuss "Mormonism" with a Latter-day Saint, I was thrilled. However, to discuss the beliefs was one thing; to become a Latter-day Saint was something entirely different. I had not the slightest desire to become a Mormon.

I shall never forget that day when I arrived home from work and my wife greeted me with, "Curtis, it's true!"

"What's true? What do you mean?" I asked, with a puzzled expression.

She replied, "What Johann says is true. Joseph Smith was and is a prophet. The Church of Jesus Christ has been restored in these latter days."

"How do you know this?" I inquired.

Virginia invited me to go into the living room. Sitting at the piano, she began to play. As she sang the words to the song "The Heavens Were Opened," tears welled in her eyes. I knew the message in those words was very meaningful to her. Completing the music, she turned and asked, "Doesn't it do something to you?"

I replied, "No." (The song is now meaningful to me too, because the Prophet Joseph Smith is now meaningful.)

The discussion that followed revealed that she was even thinking about being baptized into the LDS Church. I just couldn't understand why. She had always, up until then, been an intelligent, rational, thinking person. I didn't think she was being duped into something against her better judgment. I was perplexed.

At that point my attitude toward the Latter-day Saints really changed drastically. Virginia says that I became uglier and uglier. That's putting it mildly. I was hostile! I despised Mormons! I did not like what they were doing to my formerly happy home. I didn't want to see a Mormon, much less speak to one. The Griffiths next door I totally ignored. I even forbade Virginia to have any more Latter-day Saints in the house. Still she kept asking me to read some books and, if what they conveyed was not true, to explain them away. I refused to read.

One morning, while kneeling in prayer at the altar in a chapel at Lackland Air Force Base, I had an experience in which the fifth chapter of the Acts of the Apostles in the New Testament was impressed upon me vividly. The words of Gamaliel reeled me back on my heels. "If this . . . work be of men, it will come to nought: but if it be of God, ye cannot overthrow it; lest haply ye be found even to fight against God." (Acts 5:38-39.) Fight against God? Why, that was the last thing I wanted to do. I loved him and wanted to serve him. During the day those words kept ringing in my thoughts. "Why," I kept asking myself, "did I have this experience?" What was the meaning of it?

Arriving home and looking into the sparkling eyes of Virginia, I had the thoughtful questions come: "Could it be that it is the Lord's will that Virginia become a Latter-day Saint? Could it be that by my precluding her from becoming one, I am fighting God?" It was that experience that changed my attitude and led to my granting permission for her to be baptized. But although I attended her baptism and thought that Bishop Griffith said some thoughtful, perceptive words during her confirmation, I still had no desire to have anything but a passive interest in her new church at best.

Six months later orders were received reassigning me to the Air Force Academy. I was thrilled! Virginia and I discussed in depth our situation in relation to our Academy life. Virginia stated that she would be active in the Protestant program at the Air Force Academy. But she still wanted me to read about Mormonism and explain why the doctrine wasn't true.

At the Academy I managed to keep fully occupied without reading Virginia's books. I refused because I considered reading them a waste of time. But as time for General Conference approached I decided to take her there—not because I had a favorable attitude but because I could then prove to her that the LDS Church conferences were no different in substance or in spirituality from any other ecclesiastical conference.

There was one person I knew in Salt Lake City. We had first met when he had gone to Lackland Air Force Base to conduct a servicemen's conference. So I asked Elder Boyd K. Packer if it would be possible to attend General Conference. He was gracious in arranging for us to attend as his guests. I didn't realize then that the Conference would have a lasting impact on my life.

Ever bright will be the memory of the first time I saw the beloved prophet, President David O. McKay. As he entered I looked at him, and tears began to trickle down my cheeks. I was embarrassed. I was an officer in the air force, and officers just didn't go around crying when they looked at other men! I didn't want to pull out my handkerchief and wipe away my tears because then people would know I was crying. But I didn't want those right around me to see tears in my eyes. In that humiliating predicament I tried to look in another direction, but I couldn't. Something kept my eyes focused upon that wonderful man. Never before in my life had I felt that way.

Another unforgettable occasion was the evening spent in the home of Elder and Sister Packer. Several guests were present, each of whom shared a choice religious experience that had enriched his life. Truly that evening I felt the Spirit of the Lord in a very real sense.

Returning to the Air Force Academy, I kept wondering about what had happened when I saw President McKay. "Could it be that the Lord is trying to tell me something?" I pondered. "Virginia has been saying that David O. McKay is a prophet. Could it be that she is right?" Those questions kept coming back into my thoughts. Many times I had attended ecclesiastical conferences and heard different men express their various views. Afterwards, I would bow my head saying, "Would to God that someone could stand up and declare, 'Thus saith the Lord.'" Was David O. McKay the one who could say that with authority?

But I still didn't want to take the time to fulfil Virginia's request to read. Then that which did get me to read came into my life. Word had spread that Virginia had become a Latter-day Saint. Different ministerial associates would approach me with, "Tell me it isn't true—what we have heard about Virginia"; or, "Curtis, you must get Virginia back into the Methodist Church." Two chaplains expressed views that I should not be at the Air Force Academy because my wife was a Mormon. When I made references to different ministers whose wives were members of other denominations, they only responded: "That's different. Their wives are Methodist, Disciples, Episcopalian, etc. Your wife is a Mormon." One chaplain made the comment that my being a Methodist minister and being married to a Mormon was like one of our leading government officials being married to a Communist. That not only showed me the distorted and prejudicial thinking of some ministers, but it also made me painfully aware that I could no longer take lightly Virginia's joining the Church.

Up to that time I had closed my mind to studying the LDS doctrines. Now the situation was different. I decided to read everything I could get my hands on. I read both LDS books and anti-Mormon books. The reason for the intensified study was two-fold: first, if Mormonism were not true, I wanted to get Virginia out of that mess; second, if it were true I wanted to know for myself and to join with her.

I must admit that the more I read anti-Mormon literature the more convinced I became that either those writers were grossly ignorant of what Latter-day Saints really believe or else they were intentionally malicious and wanted to distort the thinking of the reader.

During my period of inquiry I had the assistance of two dedicated Latter-day Saints who were remarkably knowledgeable in the gospel—Merrill Bateman, an economics professor, and Bishop Leroy Gunnell, an English professor at the Academy. Not only could they discuss theology on a very rational, logical level, but they also deeply impressed me with their spirituality and their sincere love for the Savior. Additionally, I had brotherly kindness such as I had never experienced before shown me daily by Earl Watson, who later baptized me. In truth, it seemed that every Saint in the Colorado Springs Second Ward showed special concern for me.

As a result of the concentrated study effort, when the time came around for the next general conference I felt impelled to attend—that time, alone. During this second visit to Salt Lake City I had two more choice experiences. The first came when I knelt in prayer with Elder Boyd K. Packer. When I arose from my knees, for the first time it came so clearly to me what it meant to "listen to the Spirit." I knew then what Moroni had been trying to tell me in Moroni 10:4. That Saturday evening at the priesthood session of the conference the second experience came. I had taken my place in the tabernacle. As President McKay entered, the organist began to play "We Thank Thee, O God, For a Prophet," and spontaneously voices began singing that hymn. I could sense that those thousands of male singers were truly grateful for the one whom they believed to be a living prophet. As I listened to those words being sung, my thoughts went back to the previous conference when I first looked upon President David O. McKay. My heart began to beat faster. As the session progressed my spirit was literally leaping with joy. Without any forethought, all of a sudden I turned to the person sitting next to me and said, "I'm going to join!" He looked at me with a puzzled expression. Of course he didn't know what had been happening within me.

Arriving back in Colorado Springs, I knew what I must do. With Virginia, her difficulty was not in gaining a testimony; it was in what she was going to do with it after she had it! My problem was getting a testimony. Once I had it, I knew what I must do.

I hadn't rushed into joining because I had to be sure. Why? I knew the Lord had called me to be a minister. I didn't want to turn my back on what the Lord had called me to do. There is a difference between being called of the Lord and being called of the Lord through the priesthood—and I know that difference. Now I know that all of my previous training was preparation for a greater calling he had in store for me.

Second, I loved the Methodist Church dearly. Many blessings had come to me through the Methodist Church. Two of my mother's brothers are Methodist ministers. My father was a lay minister. He had wanted to be a minister but didn't have the opportunity to prepare adequately by acquiring a formal education. He loved the Lord and spent his Sunday afternoons reading scriptures to a blind man. Virginia and I were married in a Methodist Church, and the covenants I made were valid to me. Our children had been baptized as infants in the Methodist Church. And the Methodist people, wherever I served, were precious and dear to me.

Third, I loved the air force and my job as a chaplain. I wanted ever so much to serve Heavenly Father and my country as a chaplain. Today, I enjoy many lasting friendships which were initiated while I was serving in the air force.

Because air force regulations preclude a chaplain's changing church affiliation and remaining on active duty, I had to resign my regular commission.

Even when I was checking out of the base, many interested Protestant friends asked me to call the Methodist Commission on Chaplains and the Chief of Air Force Chaplains to inform them that I had changed my mind. Many acquaintances thought I had really lost my senses when I resigned without having employment. Even though I didn't have a job, I launched out in faith. I knew that the crucial quality of discipleship is to be willing to pray in your garden of Gethsemane, "Father, let thy will be done regardless of the consequences."

Is the Church really worth what we went through? Especially when I consider particular experiences in the temple the answer is unequivocally, "Yes!" Going to the temple with my lovely wife for our own endowments and then going into the sealing room where we knelt with our precious children were experiences of incalculable worth. Going to the temple has put marriage in an entirely different perspective. For the first time I began to see marriage as an integral part of an eternal progression. I didn't think it was humanly possible to love my wife more than I did. And yet, after having gone to the temple my feelings and love for her have grown beyond all expectation. The temple experiences have truly enriched our marriage and have drawn us closer together. I now know that any Latter-day Saint youth who does not plan and prepare for a temple marriage is selling his birthright for a mess of pottage.

Another powerfully moving experience came when I went to the temple to do the work for a person who is very dear to me—a man who died shortly before I entered the first grade. I prepared for a long time to be worthy for that occasion. When I came up out of the water, after being baptized in his behalf, I felt that I wasn't alone—that the person very dear to me was also there. Later, at a particular place in the temple, I knew it wasn't just my imagination. Something marvelous happened. When I left the temple that day I knew my father was alive. I knew that he had been waiting for that day. I knew that he was grateful. On that day in the temple I gained knowledge and a certainty that I could never have acquired in aeons of reading books on systematic theology or philosophy. There are many things I do not know, but these things I do know: there is life beyond the experience we call death, and those living on the other side of the veil are identifiable, as they were in mortal life.

I am reluctant to describe in more detail those precious experiences which I have mentioned, not because they are secret but because they are sacred.

As a Latter-day Saint I have answers to specific questions that I never would have had answers to otherwise. It is no longer "I think" or "perhaps" or "it might be" or "I hope"; it is "I know." This pertains to questions such as:

What is the nature of the Godhead?

Is the Holy Spirit a personage or just a description of an existential experience?

Did I exist in some form prior to this mortal existence?

In what way are spirits and resurrected beings identifiable?

What does it mean to be made in the image and likeness of God?

Also, many passages in the Bible now make sense, whereas previously their meanings were open to speculation or perhaps had to be explained away as the work of later editorialists. A few examples of these are:

When the morning stars sang together and all the sons of God shouted for joy. (Job 38:7.)

Before I formed thee in the belly I knew thee; and before thou camest forth out of the womb I sanctified thee, and I ordained thee a prophet unto the nations. (Jeremiah 1:5.)

And the graves were opened; and many bodies of the saints which slept arose, and came out of the graves after his resurrection, and went into the holy city, and appeared unto many. (Matthew 27:52-53.)

And other sheep I have, which are not of this fold: them also I must bring, and they shall hear my voice; and there shall be one fold, and one shepherd. (John 10:16.)

[Jesus] called of God an high priest after the order of Melchizedec. (Hebrews 5:10.)

To those Latter-day Saints whose lives touched mine in guiding me to this, the Savior's restored Church, I will be eternally gratefully. Because their joy was to share the gospel with others, my family and I today enjoy the blessings of the gospel.

I bear solemn witness that God the Father lives, that Jesus is the Christ, that this is his work in which we are engaged in these latter days, that we can be guided by the Spirit, that through the acceptance of the Savior's atoning sacrifice and through the principle of obedience we can return to the Father's presence in an exalted state. And I do so in the name of the Lord Jesus Christ. Amen.

Aasmund Johansen

FROM DEATH UNTO LIFE

Far up in the northernmost quarter of Norway, in the university city and fishing and whaling center of Tromsö, lives an insurance executive named Aasmund Johansen.

Admired as a successful professional man, he is unsurpassed in Norway as a layman respected for his religious convictions. He is the presiding elder of the Tromsö Branch of The Church of Jesus Christ of Latter-day Saints, a member of the Trondheim District Council, and a missionary for the Church par excellence. In fact, he has been instrumental in so many conversions and is so thorough in the fellowshiping of new members that some affectionately refer to him as "Apostle Paul of the North."

By his daily actions he emulates the scripture: "For I am not ashamed of the gospel of Christ: for it is the power of God unto salvation to every one that believeth. . . ." (Romans 1:16.)

Former Norway mission president Ray Johnson admires Brother Johansen for his knowledge and understanding of the gospel, his great faith, his deep devotion, and his fervent testimony. Says President Johnson: "In areas where he has presided, Brother Johansen has been like a good shepherd carefully looking after his flock."

Strangely, if it had not been for a savage, nearly fatal attack upon his life, Brother Johansen might be just another average person.

On the largest island in Norway, close to the Arctic Circle, I was born the next to the youngest in a family of six children. This was just before the Second World War broke out. My mother, a member of the Norwegian Lutheran State Church, baptized me when I was but a few days old. She was afraid that I was going to die. This belief that unless a deceased child was christened before he died he cannot be saved was one of the reasons why I came into opposition with the state church and its teachings.

I am very grateful that my mother taught me to pray, and this I did often. When I attended high school and was indoctrinated in the teachings of the state church, I often found myself in arguments with the minister-teacher concerning important doctrines. At that time of my life, whenever I had difficulties or whenever I tried to solve the many perplexing problems of life by my own reasoning, I often felt confused. I remember praying for a convincing confirmation of God's existence. I had many experiences in my youth which confirmed to me that there was a God. My great problem was that there were so many churches and sects, all teaching their own doctrines. I felt the confusion, and I had no affiliation with any one of them in particular.

In February of 1969 something happened to me that was to alter my life. At the time my soul was in turmoil, and I cried often at night to God. I had an ominous feeling that something serious was about to happen. One of my friends also thought that something serious was going to happen to me or someone in the family.

On February 16 an acquaintance attacked me in my home. I was first stabbed in the back and then, afterwards, received twenty knife wounds in my chest and arms. A friend who was present was also stabbed but escaped by running away.

When I realized that my life was coming to an end, I cried with my last bit of strength: "Jesus Christ, help me!" As I did so, it seemed as if the evil spirit departed from my attacker. He threw the knife away and drove me to the hospital. There my condition was determined to be very critical, and I was sent to a larger hospital by helicopter. I did not expect to live. Petitioning my Heavenly Father, I said: "If I live through this, I promise to go in whatever direction you will show me."

After having been more dead than alive for several days, I now quickly responded to treatment. I was released from that hospital after three weeks, and was transferred to Oslo for further treatment.

Shortly after I had arrived there I called home and announced that I had decided to seek God. Friends and family asked me what church I intended to join, and my answer was that I didn't know yet whether it was even necessary to join any church. I would not make any decision before God convinced me which way to go. I was determined to do his will.

That same evening I went to my room to pray to God and ask him if he would show me where I should go—would he please reveal it to me. Immediately the thought struck me that I should go to a certain place to see some people I had not seen for a while.

After I had told these acquaintances of my experiences, they in turn explained to me about the church they belonged to —the Mormon Church. They awakened my interest to the point that I went with them to a conference in Drammen the next Sunday. This was my first contact with the Mormon Church, of which I had heard scarcely anything before, and I was very apprehensive and much afraid that my being in attendance at that particular church would turn out to be a gross mistake. As I stood on the steps to the meetinghouse I felt an urge to turn around and leave, but when I arrived inside and felt the sweet spirit that was there I could already feel the dawning of a testimony that this was the true Church and that I was moving in the right direction. A meeting with two missionaries was arranged so that I could receive the discussions.

At this same time I sought opportunities to hear and to converse with ministers of other churches in Oslo. I can recall that one of them who strongly advised me against joining the Mormon Church said: "You can join any other church without offense—why not the Baptists? The Methodists? The Presbyterians? If you don't feel at home in the state church, join one of these, but the Mormons!—no, that is heresy and you must be very careful." It surprised me that he suggested other churches than his own, and in fact he would have settled for any other church but The Church of Jesus Christ of Latter-day Saints.

I soon found out that I must continue to rely on God for unbiased and wise guidance. Every night after having received lessons from the missionaries, I went into the forest outside Oslo and prayed to God that he would manifest to me whether their teachings were true. As a result he did manifest this truth to me. There was no doubt in my mind when on the sixth of June, 1969, I accepted the challenge from the missionaries and was baptized. It was a happy day; the most joyous day I had had in my life up to then.

I have received many blessings and much happiness since I was baptized. I have seen many of my friends baptized into the Church, among them the friend who was struck down with me on that awful night. I have experienced in particular the truth of the words of Nephi: ". . . I know that the Lord giveth no commandments unto the children of men, save he shall prepare a way for them that they may accomplish the thing which he commandeth them." (1 Nephi 3:7.) A way has always been opened to me when I have been confronted with difficulties. An example is the time I was sent up north to live in a place where there were no members. I prayed to God, and shortly thereafter the mission president sent two missionaries to me. I was allowed to labor with them for a couple of years. This experience strengthened and developed me.

I had been a member of the Church for only eleven months when I was ordained an elder and assigned to preside over the northernmost congregation in the Church—in Hammerfest, the northernmost incorporated city in the world. I again approached God: "Thou hast commanded me to marry, and I surely need a faithful woman at my side. Please, Father, show her to me." It did not take long before a beautiful young girl was baptized into the Church in Hammerfest. God showed me that she was to be my wife, but the problem was that she did not seem to be of the same opinion. I challenged her to ask God. After a while she came back to me and said: "I have asked God and I feel that he has answered me that I am to have you." We went to the United States, where we were sealed for time and all eternity in the Salt Lake Temple on June 29, 1972. This was the greatest blessing I had received from God since being baptized into the Church.

I know from the bottom of my heart that Jesus is the Christ, God's living Son, and that The Church of Jesus Christ of Latter-day Saints is the kingdom of God on the earth. I bear this testimony in all humility and in the name of Jesus Christ. Amen.

WANG TIEN TE

TAIWAN CONGREGATION FOLLOWS TEEN-AGER

"The meek will he guide in judgment: and the meek will he teach his way." (Psalm 25:9.)

About twenty years ago in Taiwan, Wang Tien Te[1] decided not to affiliate himself with any church but to start one of his own. He chose to teach the gospel strictly from the Bible. His wife worked by his side in the small church they built in front of their little house.

From the Bible Wang taught his flock many truths, including tithing, study of scripture, daily prayer, abstinence of all things harmful to the body, and baptism by immersion. He was their shepherd.

One day Wang and his family learned that their fifteen-year-old Julie (Ju Ling) was interested in a new religion. She had been moved upon by the Spirit to learn about the restoration of the gospel.

Julie's courage in her "little sixteen years," as she charmingly expresses it, and her parents' wisdom shine through the two simple narratives of father and daughter. They represent some of the finest examples of conversions to the gospel in the latter days.

God has always given responsibility to common people so that their faith can be tested. I am just a common man, a faithful member of the Church. I have had a most unusual life. I have nine children whom I have provided for with my own two hands,

---

[1]Brother Wang and daughter Julie's stories were made available by President Malan Jackson and staff of the Taiwan Mission and Mrs. Truman (Ann) Madsen, personal friend of Julie Wang.

assisted by God's kindness. My only schooling was six years' basic education in an elementary school.

Through enthusiasm and faith in the Lord I led the members of my church in K'o Liao to live God's commandments. At times, however, I found myself feeling empty. I do not know exactly how to describe that feeling. I did know, however, that God loved me and that he would give me what I needed.

Through the power of God, my youngest daughter Julie was led to the true Church. Since her conversion, my family, myself, and the members of my little church have found the fulness of the true gospel of Jesus Christ.

Because of the biased comments I had heard from people who were against the Mormon Church, when I first saw the Book of Mormon in Julie's hands I became very upset with her. Julie cried after I scolded her. But I forbade her to touch the Book of Mormon again. Her eyes were full of tears as she quietly said to me: "Father, I love you very much and I respect you. I do not want you to hurt me. I can tell you that I have found the true Church and the true gospel. I was not told by man. I was moved upon by the Spirit of the Lord and I have to insist that I know this is God's true Church. I know that only through this Church can I go back to my Heavenly Father's presence. Father, please do not stop me!"

I was very surprised that she was so firm. She had never talked to me like that before. She had changed greatly—from an innocent little girl who did not know anything to a mature girl who knew what she was talking about. Her testimony at that time did have some influence on me.

Before very long, she brought her baptismal application form to me to be signed. I spoke sharply to her without any feeling for her desire. I wanted her to join my church, but she refused. She said: "Father, I will not accept baptism without authority. I have to be baptized into the true Church, through the power of the priesthood. God wants me to join the true Church. He wants to save me. Please let me go along that narrow path and receive the baptism of water and of the Holy Ghost. I beg you to ask God whether this Church is true or not. He will answer your prayers."

Again, I was astonished. She was only fifteen years old. Fifteen! Where did she get the courage to tell me that? For two whole days she hid herself in her room. She did not eat anything during those two days. She was constantly praying. I was moved.

Then I picked up the Book of Mormon and I found that I liked it. I began to ask God. Time after time I asked. I came to realize that it was time for my whole family and all the members of my church to receive the blessings of the true gospel. I finally understood that what I really needed was authority from God. Since joining the Church I have received that authority, the holy priesthood. It is indeed a blessing from God. I am very grateful for it.

I want to bear my testimony that only through God's true Church and his authority can we see him again. I know that the Church is led by a living prophet who receives revelations from God for our guidance I know that the Book of Mormon is the word of God. I testify to these things in the name of Jesus Christ. Amen.

Julie's Story

God loves us, regardless of what class of people we are. We are all his sons and daughters. Heavenly Father gave us our marvelous physical bodies and a chance to be tested upon this earth that we might progress.

I was born in a country village by the sea. My father was a pastor of the only Protestant church in the village. I have eight brothers and sisters. I'm the youngest. From birth I was raised in this Christian family and learned to obey God's commandments. I became familiar with many Bible stories.

From the time I was small I always enjoyed strolling to the seaside near my home and to the nearby potato fields to think. I remember that when I was small I would go with schoolmates, but in later years I liked to go alone. I can remember always respecting and loving nature. Like other children, I always felt happy to attend school, to go to the seashore to play in the sand, and to chase in the fields. I saw that life was good—beautiful flowers, the reflection of the evening sun upon the ocean, pretty little cliff swallows, and the fields of waving rice. My eyes did not see that which was evil and ugly. Not once did I travel out of the K'o Liao countryside. My childhood was very happy.

When I was thirteen years old I went for the first time to the provincial capital city of Kao Hsiung, there to attend junior high school. For the first time I saw life in a big city setting. I saw the various shapes and colors, the flowers and greenery of the city. I watched the people a little timidly. I went into a bookstore, and there I came to realize what a great many books there are in the city. I formed the habit of reading, and whenever I had time I would take books into the country or to the beach and read those things to help answer my questions about religion. I was very interested in this subject, and the books seemed to help me to understand more about Christianity. It was only later that I learned that those things were the ideas of men and did not contain the true religion.

I was there in that city for only a year before I switched to a school in the country nearer my home. When I was fifteen, however, I found myself back in Kao Hsiung working.

One hot summer evening I went out on the city street for a walk to enjoy the breezes, since there was no cool seashore or potato fields to walk to. When I got to the pedestrian crossover I found that two young American men were passing out papers. Walking by, I took one just for fun. I didn't even notice what the paper said, but putting it in my pocket I went on my way and finished my walk. Upon returning home I pulled the slip of paper out of my pocket and was startled by what I read on a line of the paper: "Why does man live upon this earth?" My interest was suddenly aroused. Yes, I wanted to know the answer to that question. I immediately mailed the paper back to the missionaries, giving my name and address.

A few days later the two missionaries came to visit me. Over the course of several weeks they taught me the gospel, helped me to recognize the true Church of Jesus Christ, and gave me answers to my questions about the purpose of life.

At that time my friends and schoolmates saw me carrying a Book of Mormon and knew I was attending the Mormon Church. They were very surprised. Some laughed at me, while others scolded me for being associated with the Church. They said things like: "You shouldn't be doing this." "How can you desert your own father's church and attend the Mormon Church?" "Don't you know the Mormon Church is evil?" They gave me a tract to read which criticized the Church. They even reviled the Church. They threatened to tell my family what I was doing.

Later my father and mother learned of my activity in the Mormon Church. My mother was heartbroken and tearfully forbade me to attend the Church any more. My father was angry with me. My brothers and sisters also scolded me. It was a time of great sadness and trouble for me.

I continued to be opposed from all sides, but God blessed me with a faith stronger than the opposition. When I came home late from work each night, when everyone was asleep, I would always kneel in prayer and cry to Heavenly Father, begging him to send me help and give me a testimony assuring me of the truthfulness of the Book of Mormon and The Church of Jesus Christ of Latter-day Saints.

One night I felt especially sad because of continued opposition from those who were nearest to me. My soul communicated a more fervent yearning for the help of the Lord and for a testimony of his truth. At that time I experienced a warm feeling in my heart such as I had never felt before. I knew it was the Holy Ghost filling my heart. With its arrival I felt no more anguish. My sorrows were dispersed. How great is the power of the Holy Ghost! This subtle yet overpowering feeling of love upon my heart was the Lord comforting my suffering soul. And finally I knew what the Lord would have me do.

The next day I met with the elders. I informed them of my testimony experience. My knowledge of the gospel continued to grow with each lesson they taught me. Fasting and prayer were tools I used often—sometimes with the participation of the elders but more often on my own. I learned that before the Lord will grant us a great blessing he first gives us a great test.

One day (a day I was fasting) during lunch break, instead of resting as usual, I went out on the street for a walk. That day the elders were fasting with me. I was surprised to suddenly see my mother seated on a bus at a nearby bus stop. When she saw me she was also surprised, and she waved me onto the bus. I quickly boarded the bus and rode home with her. It was like a miracle to run into my mother in this way. Also I just happened to have my baptismal application papers with me.

On the bumpy bus going home I begged my mother to sign the papers giving consent for me to be baptized. I was so weary that I kept falling asleep, but I would again awaken and persist in asking for her permission to be baptized. She tried to get me to rest but I would not. It amazed her to see the determination of her child. But she told me she had been moved by my unwavering faith of the previous three-and-a-half months. She didn't oppose my wishes any longer, but instead comforted me. She told me she had been giving this matter much thought and prayer herself during the past few days and knew now that what I desired was the will of the Lord. Mother was now able to take her pen and sign her name giving consent to my baptism.

When my father knew of this he became angry. He wanted to baptize me himself. I drummed up my courage and then bore a firm testimony to my father.

In the end God won. His power slowly changed my father's heart. On August 19, 1972, I was baptized a member of The Church of Jesus Christ of Latter-day Saints at the Kao Hsiung chapel. Afterward, the Lord led my father into his true Church, along with my family and the greater part of my father's congregation. They all received God's blessing of baptism and the gift of the Holy Ghost under the hands of bearers of the true priesthood of God.

In conclusion I want to leave my witness. I very much appreciate this beautiful opportunity to tell everyone the testimony of my inner heart. I now know the true gospel of Jesus Christ.

I know that God restored this gospel and his true Church—The Church of Jesus Christ of Latter-day Saints— through the Prophet Joseph Smith. I know that God leads this Church through a living prophet today. The Bible and the Book of Mormon contain the word of God, which help us to better understand his gospel. I know that a person has to obey God's commandments to obtain true happiness. And I know from my own experience that if we but ask God he will surely help us and care for us.

F. WOODWORTH WHITLOCK, JR.

PAYING THE PRICE

A young American minister in Uruguay, deeply concerned about his flock, was told by a distinguished Latter-day Saint: "One of these days you'll be a Mormon."

Years later, F. Woodworth Whitlock, Jr., alone in his study, struggled with truth day after day. If the book he held in his hands withstood his analytical probing, the price he would have to pay for receiving such knowledge could be extremely high—the loss of career and the almost certain loss of wife and family.

Many years before, as a young sailor, he had made the decision that if "God is real he should get my total devotion." God had never been so real as now, nor the purpose of life so clearly defined. But where was the strength he needed?

> *"He that loveth father or mother more than me is not worthy of me: and he that loveth son or daughter more than me is not worthy of me. And he that taketh not his cross, and followeth after me, is not worthy of me." (Matthew 10:37-38.)*

The way Woodworth Whitlock handled the situation becomes a vivid demonstration of how the Lord would have us meet what might seem to be insurmountable difficulties.

Since Mother and Dad had been raised in the Baptist Church, it was natural that the four of us children should be too. I well remember the Sunday morning (I was about ten years old) when my Sunday School teacher asked me if I wanted to be baptized— by immersion—and to receive Jesus Christ as my personal Lord and Savior and become a member of the Baptist Church. I loved and trusted this man enough to know that that was what I wanted to do. The night I was baptized into the Baptist Church was a very precious experience to me because it was my own first step towards Jesus Christ.

As I moved into high school, however, I began to lose interest in the things of God and soon religion just faded out of my life completely. I became sick of going to Sunday School just to please my parents and fed up with pretending. I was far more concerned about my girl and my car than I was about "any old Bible stories."

By the time I was halfway through college, I just didn't know what I was living for. I concluded: "I've got to get away from all this—from family and friends, church, school, the whole business—and get out into the world and find out what, if anything, really is worth living for."

In my desperation I quit school and joined the navy, and that did get me away from almost everything—except school. The navy sent me right back to electronics school for a year and it was almost too much for me because I had no more heart for studying. Eventually I was assigned to duty aboard ship, and that ship became my home for the next three years. It was during those years, operating out of the naval base at Norfolk, Virginia, cruising up and down and across the Atlantic, that I had the opportunity to begin to explore new areas of life. For one thing, I browsed in bookstores, picking up books on philosophy and religion. I found myself hungering to read what other men had to say about the purpose of life, the meaning of death, suffering, war, etc.

At this time too I began to visit different churches, including the Catholic Church and Jewish synagogues. Then I found my way into a big Methodist Church in downtown Norfolk where there was a wonderful Sunday evening program for the young people (much like our LDS youth program). The church was operated and attended by people who seemed to have a real knowledge and love of Jesus Christ. The minister of this church took me into his home as though I were a member of his own family, and his family's genuine love and his fatherly interest were a great blessing to me.

It also happened that at this time I became acquainted with various Methodist missionaries, couples on their way to Africa or S.E. Asia, and young people just returned from South America. One I came to be especially fond of was an elderly lady, white-haired and crippled with arthritis. She came to church faithfully every Sunday using a cane, making her way up to a seat near the front. Unmarried, she had spent all of her life serving the Lord as a missionary in China. When the missionaries were run out of China by the Communists, she spent her last missionary years in Cuba. Now she was retired and just waiting to be called home by the Lord. We often spent several hours together of a Sunday afternoon, when she would talk of her experiences as a missionary. It was obvious to me that she had a spirit and a purpose that I lacked—and wanted. By comparison I was empty inside, and I recognized this.

Contacts like this and reading about men who had found some answer to their lives through religious service began to open my mind to new ideas. One thought in particular began to force its way in on my thinking. It was this: If God is real at all, he's *the most important thing of all!* I couldn't escape the relentless logic of this thought. Yet I wasn't comfortable with it because, as I've already indicated, several other things had already gained a great hold on my life and had become more important to me than God. For all that, I couldn't get away from the thought that, if God is real, he should get my total devotion; if he's not, I should forget God and all that is said in Bibles and churches.

This kind of black or white logic forced me finally to the decision that I would give God my whole life through the ministry. At first it was a frightening idea to me because I had never envisioned myself as a black-robed preacher pounding a pulpit on Sunday—far from it. As I considered how I might serve God, I thought: "What the churches in this country need isn't more preachers, but less people. Get the people out of the churches and into the world preaching the gospel! That's the best thing that could happen to the churches!"

So I wrote to the Board of Missions of the Methodist Church and told them I wanted to be a missionary. They wrote back and congratulated me on my good decision, and then explained that first of all I should plan to go back and finish college when I got out of the navy, since all of their missionaries are college graduates. After college, if I planned to be a minister, I would have to attend a graduate school of theology for at least three years before being ordained.

While I was eager to get right out into the mission field as soon as possible, I determined to go through with the five or six years of preparation required. I concluded, "If this job is worth doing at all, it is worth doing the right way, no matter what it costs or how long it takes." Furthermore, I realized that if I was really serious about being a missionary I didn't have to wait until I was out in the mission field. I had helped bring enough of my buddies aboard ship after a lost weekend to know that if I really was serious about religion I could start to work right where I was. And indeed I did have some grand experiences with shipmates—discussions, worship services, Bible study groups, evening prayers aboard ship—as well as in the churches and missions I visited ashore. Then as soon as I was discharged from the navy, I went down to Mexico to join a group of Methodist college students from the U.S. They were taking part in a work project in the mountains, building a camp for some of the youth of Mexico. This would provide an opportunity to see if foreign missionary work was what I really wanted or if I was just kidding myself.

When I joined this group of twenty-four American students, I found there were half a dozen girls among them, one of whom also wanted to be a missionary. We quickly struck up a friendship and soon felt we were just right for each other. After just a few days I was sent on a separate assignment to Mexico City with a smaller group of boys, while all the girls in the work camp remained with the main body up in the mountains of Monterrey. We wrote many letters back and forth, however, and by the end of the summer Betty and I had decided to get married and spend our lives together as missionaries.

In the years that followed I finished college and went on to graduate school at Northwestern University in Chicago, where the Methodist Church has one of its largest seminaries. For three years we studied the Bible, theology, church administration, psychology, and all the things that were thought necessary in order for us to be effective ministers of the gospel. We were seeking God's answers to man's problems. The final stage of our preparation took us to San Jose, Costa Rica, where we spent nine months with missionaries of other denominations in full-time study of the Spanish language. Then, at long last, in January of 1961, Betty and I arrived at our first full-time assignment in the mission field. It was in South America in the little country of Uruguay, far down on the south side, tucked in between the giant countries of Argentina and Brazil.

The particular church we were assigned to was located in the meat packing district of the capital city of Montevideo. It was a large, modern building with chapel, recreation hall, classrooms, library, kitchen, basketball court, and showers. Adjacent to the property was a big new Goodwill Industries building where handicapped people were employed in repairing discarded items for resale. In the church itself there was an established social center with weekday classes and cultural events for the people of the neighborhood. Altogether it seemed to me to be an overwhelming opportunity for serving people and witnessing to the love of God in an area that really needed such service.

I decided to begin with the youth of the church. As it happened, they had already organized a summer campout, with all the details of scheduled activities, food, work assignments, discussion groups, etc., already arranged. All I had to do was go along and enjoy what they were doing. What they were doing, however, turned out to be Communist training, with the organized discussions focused on social-political issues. When I attempted to relate the gospel as I understood it to the things they were discussing, they would reply: "But the gospel has been in the world for two thousand years and the world is as badly off today as it ever was. If that's the way the gospel works, it really isn't very effective, is it?" They pointed to countries like the United States that has had Christianity for over two hundred years and has preached it to the world. They said: "Look at America's juvenile delinquency and racial prejudice and political policies overseas—how selfish! If this is the way your gospel works, you can keep it! What we want are changes that are long overdue!" They pointed to nations that were bringing changes to large segments of their population and argued: "Now, these revolutionary countries have their problems, sure, but at least they're doing things and bringing changes that have been needed for a long time. They're not just talking or preaching sweet Sunday School sermons."

Now, I appreciated the passion for change in the hearts of these young people. They wanted to put things right in the world. But Satan also operates with a tremendous passion, and if we don't have a greater passion for righteousness we'll never beat him. The right kind of passion must be motivated by God, and it must be unselfish. In my opinion, those young people were motivated by bitterness, criticism and a sense of superiority. This was pretty rocky soil for the gospel. I was convinced that the only way you can ever put the world right is by beginning where you are, with your own life, but that isn't where they wanted to begin. They wanted to begin with the other man and the other nation.

After such experiences with the youth, I decided, "If this is the way it is with the young people here, I'll have to start somewhere else." I examined the church register and looked up the names of the older members of the church. Most of them weren't in church on Sunday and I thought I'd go and see why. As I visited with them individually in their homes, they would often say things like: "Well, every time I go to church they ask for money"; or "Once I went to church and Sister So-and-So said such-and-such, and if that's the way Christians are, I'm never going back!"

I found that every time I came out of a house after such a visit, I felt more burdened. But I reasoned: "That's what I came down here for: to preach and pray and visit; to plant and plow and cultivate. I came to do the Lord's work; and if the harvest doesn't happen to come during my time here, that's no worry of mine." The Lord would bring the harvest in due time if the people would be faithful. I knew this because I had seen people who had taken God seriously and their lives had been changed. That's what got me started in the whole business anyway. So, I kept at it.

But all at once my life got a little more complicated. I began to notice dark-suited young men going up and down the street in pairs knocking on all the doors. It was the invasion of the Mormons!

I didn't mind it at first, but one Sunday at church a sister said to me: "Pastor, it's just awful—the Mormons came to my house this week, and when they got inside they wouldn't leave for anything. How do you get rid of them?"

I didn't like that at all. To begin with, I thought, that's just plain rude. If you're a guest in someone's house (and an uninvited guest at that) and you don't have the courtesy to know when to leave, you've got some Christian manners to learn. Even more important, I didn't think anybody had a right to enter the home of a family who had already made a basic commitment to Jesus Christ and confuse them about religion. The most important thing you can ever do with your life I reasoned, is commit it completely to Jesus Christ, and basically that's what these people had done. Whether they were Methodist or Baptist or Catholic, it didn't matter. The main thing they had done when they had joined their church (if it's Christian) was commit their lives to Christ. There might be a lot of other differences, but they were secondary. The main thing is Jesus Christ.

If these Mormon missionaries didn't appreciate what accepting Christ meant, it was my job to help them to understand what they had done and to live by it. Here are these kids, I thought, coming out of Salt Lake City with a high-powered sales pitch about Joseph Smith and a bunch of gold plates (that conveniently disappeared so that nobody could prove a thing), and they pass this off as the latest thing in religion. To make it even more delicious and interesting, they dress it all up and cover it over with a frosting of basketball and baseball and dances. Of course, everybody likes to play games and join the club until they find out what the Mormons want them to believe.

Anyway, I thought, if they want to tackle somebody, why don't they try some of the Communists or atheists? There were three million people down there in Uruguay, most of whom did not have faith in Jesus Christ. The Mormons should try some of those who didn't have any faith instead of going around confusing some of those who had already made a beginning. Certainly there were enough people down there to occupy all of us missionaries full-time and still have people left over. And if I ever got the chance, I thought, I would tell these fellows, not in a spirit of antagonism but very frankly, that we ought to learn to work together. Other churches were trying to bridge the differences and focus on Christ, and to me that was the right thing to do. If we couldn't get along down here, we'd never be together "up there,". that's for sure!

I was sitting in my study one day when the doorbell rang. I half expected to find yet another beggar at the door, but instead, there were two big, grinning Mormon missionaries— right at my own front door! "Some audacity to come calling on a minister!" I thought. "They don't care who they call on!" One of them said, in kind of a foolish voice, "We'd like to come in and look around and learn a little bit about the Methodist Church"—as if he was shopping for a new religion. Well, I knew he wasn't, but he had to say something, so I let the two young men in. My thought was: "I won't be rude. I'll be friendly, because that's the Christian way to be, and I'll see if we can bridge some of the differences between us and do the thing that will build unity in the name of Christ. Uruguay and the whole world needs a united witness from people who believe in Christ."

I invited the fellows in and showed them all around the building. I could almost see them licking their chops. I thought: "They'd like to move in and take over, or at least pick off a few easy members if they could." The Mormons met up the street, where they crowded into a little, dingy, damp building which was just bulging at the seams already. After I had shown the missionaries around, we sat down in my office. They asked me, "How is the Methodist Church organized, and how does it run?" I thought, "Man, what ignorance! These kids must live in a cave. The Methodists are one of the biggest Protestant churches in the world." Of course, I didn't know anything about the Mormons, but I was sure they were nobody—just a little group off in Utah; one of many small sects in the world today.

I told the young men something about the origin of the Methodist Church, about John Wesley and what a great man of God he was, and they seemed to understand and appreciate it. To my relief, they did not raise the subject of religion to argue about it. I was really grateful for this because I didn't want to argue religion with anybody. I wasn't down there in Uruguay for that. There had been too much of that in the world already. Furthermore, to my even greater delight, these fellows up and left and I didn't have to throw them out as I thought I would.

The next time they came there had been a change in companions; but then they were always changing and rotating elders. It seemed they had an endless supply—I didn't know where they got them all. In fact, the change in companions was often their excuse to come calling. They'd come to the door every month or so like Fuller Brush men, and they'd say: "Pastor, this is Elder So-and-So from Idaho. He's the latest arrival to the branch. We thought you'd like to meet him." They acted as if I was branch president or something. I couldn't care less who was the new arrival to the branch, but I realized this was their gimmick for coming to see me. Since they never argued religion, we always stayed on a friendly basis.

During this time a couple of remarkable things happened to me in connection with the Mormons. I was a member of the Rotary Club, having been invited to join the local chapter largely on the merits of my predecessor, a missionary who had pioneered in that area and for thirty years had done a great work in the neighborhood. Out of appreciation for him, I was invited to take his place. Because the Mormons were making quite an impact in the area, the program chairman arranged for them to speak at one of our dinner meetings. The speaker was the mission president, President J. Thomas Fyans, a successful businessman from the U.S.

When the meeting was over, the Mormon missionaries (elders) motioned me to come over and meet their hero. I was determined I wasn't going to be impressed. If he's a good man, that's fine, I thought. I'd met good men before. President Fyans is a tall, lean man; very gracious and soft-spoken. When they introduced me, he leaned over and said: "Now, you ought to listen to what these boys have to say. They've got something really special and important for you." That set me off a little bit, and I responded, "Well, we're all serving the same Lord, aren't we?" "Yes, that's right," he replied, "we are, but still you ought to give them a hearing." And then he looked me straight in the eye and said, "One of these days you'll be a Mormon." That really set me off, and I said, "Well, if the Lord ever says so."

I didn't think any more about that encounter then, but I had another experience that I did think about and couldn't shake off. As I looked over the church register for names and addresses of all the people who weren't coming to church, so I could call on them, I noticed the name of a young girl I'd never met. I asked some of the members about her and was told she had joined the Mormons before I came. It was too bad, they added, because she was one of the finest young girls the Methodist Church had, and the church couldn't afford to lose its best young people.

I wondered why she had left her name on the Methodist register. If she were now a member of another church, she ought to ask for a transfer. She couldn't be a Methodist and a Mormon at the same time. I decided to call on her and find out for myself just how she did feel. Maybe she had gone over to the Mormons, found out some of their ideas, and now missed the plain, simple Bible doctrine and fellowship of her Methodist friends; and yet she'd be humiliated to admit that she'd made a foolish mistake. I would just go and invite her back if she wanted to come back and assure her that she would be perfectly welcome. On the other hand, if she was happy where she was, that was fine with me; but we ought to clear it up.

I went over to her house and knocked on the door. She answered the door and I explained: "I'm the new pastor. I've come to call and see how things are." She invited me in and we sat around the living room table with her mother. Right away she explained, not defensively but very calmly and humbly, "Mom and I have joined the LDS Church, and we're really happy. We don't go to the movies every Sunday as we used to, because in the morning there's Sunday School and in the afternoon we go back for sacrament meeting; and then all week we're thinking what a wonderful time we had at church Sunday and how wonderful it's going to be next Sunday." Well, I was just thrilled with the tremendous spirit in that home. This was exactly what I had been looking for; what I had come to help build up in the lives of the people I served. Here was someone that really loved the Lord and his Church. For once, there were no gripes and complaints. Nothing for me to be burdened with here. I didn't have a thing to give this girl and her mother. I was completely uplifted; there was no other way to describe it.

We had prayer together, and as I left I said, "I hope you'll pray for the Methodists that they'll catch this same wonderful spirit." Not that they'd join her church necessarily; just that they'd get that same spirit that she had.

As I walked home, I thought, it doesn't really matter what kind of weird doctrine a church comes up with; if it can do *that* for people, it's all right. And until I could do better, I just didn't have anything to complain about concerning the Mormons. When I returned to my office, I made a note in the church register removing the girl from membership. Then, in a separate notebook I kept, on the page where her name appeared, I wrote simply: "Lost to the Methodists, won to Christ." It was obvious to me what she had found, and I was thrilled.

I thought a lot about that incident and from that time on I was less fearful of the Mormons. I wasn't interested in learning more, because the little that I had heard or knew about Mormon beliefs was too far-out from the familiar principles of the gospel I knew to be of any interest to me. I was glad, however, for what the Mormons had been able to do for this girl. In fact,

I knew several others they were welcome to try on, since I wasn't able to do as well.

After I had been working in Montevideo for about two years, I found myself spiritually exhausted. I just didn't have a thing more to give. I don't suppose I could have gotten up in the pulpit one more Sunday. I had poured out everything that I knew and believed about the gospel. That's how much there was in me —it was all gone in two years. Furthermore, there was not a single person in our church so far as I knew who could stand up and say, "I know Jesus Christ lives today in the flesh, and I'll be with him to see him and live with him some day." Not one person. I couldn't even say it for sure myself at that point. I didn't want to quit on the Lord, because I had given my life to God in all seriousness and sincerity. I had promised that I would serve him, no questions asked, for as long as he might choose. I didn't care what came, neither was I looking for success; but at the same time I didn't have a thing more to give—and I knew he knew that I didn't.

During this difficult period I happened to be reading in the field of psychology, and suddenly it seemed to be that here was the answer for me; that psychology held the key to explain all my thoughts and actions, even my religious ones. I began to give serious thought to leaving the ministry and the church and returning to the U.S. for further training and personal counseling. In this way I hoped to be able to help others more realistically and more effectively than I had been able to do up to that point. I no longer knew *what* I believed about God or prayer, and I no longer cared whether I ever entered a church again or not.

I prepared a carefully worded, psychologically-oriented statement of resignation, consisting of several typewritten pages, and sent copies to the parents of Betty and myself as well as to my superiors in the church. This happened to be the period when the Methodist Church held its annual business meeting and conference. It was a time for reviewing the year's accomplishments and reassigning some of the ministers to different churches. Knowing of my personal crisis, the church officials assigned me to serve a smaller church in the interior of the country. They felt this would give me a chance to get out from under the pressure of a big city and all the revolutionary agitation that I had encountered there. I considered it, and without too much struggle I decided to give it a try. Maybe this was God's second chance for me. If so, he would provide. On the other hand, if this were just more of the some old thing, it would be obvious to me right away and I would quit and go home as I had intended.

So we packed up and moved. Once we were settled in our new location, sure enough, things did seem wonderfully different. The life there was a lot simpler and slower and the people were more humble. These young people didn't have the same revolutionary preoccupation. They would come into our home every evening and we would talk about the things that were of interest to them. Then they would invite me out to the beach to play their kind of football, or I would have them help me repair an old Model A we had just acquired. In this way we were beginning to have a wonderful time together. They assured me that they weren't interested simply in parties and fun; they really wanted to learn about Christ.

About this time, guess who came calling! This time they were mobilized on bicycles, four of them. On about their second visit the Mormon missionaries brought me a book, and they showed me that it was inscribed from some missionary friends of theirs down in the capital city who had intended to give it to us. Finding that we had moved, they had sent it by way of their friends. Inside the cover was written: "To the Whitlock family, a token of our friendship"—and so on—signed Elder Gary Wood and Stewart Slingerland. Well, I never did associate the names and faces of these young fellows. I only saw them about once every month or two months, and they all looked alike to me anyway. Same suit, same tie—same tailor, I guess. But as I reflected, that name "Slingerland" did ring a bell. I remembered him to be the very timid, red-faced young man who had been sitting in my front room one evening, back in Montevideo, while his senior companion introduced him.

He was the newest arrival to the branch, and not only was he a convert to the Church but there was something else unusual about him. His senior companion explained: "He's too modest to admit it, so I'll tell you. He's an M.D." A medical doctor; he'd gone all the way through college, through medical school, even finishing his internship, and just at the time he was ready to start his practice he'd been converted to the Church. He'd dropped everything to go on a mission. I knew what this meant in the field of science because I had started off college in engineering myself. This mission would put him years behind. I was really impressed with this man's humility and dedication.

As I now saw his name in this book, I thought, "Well, these are his scriptures. They meant that much to him, so I'll take them out of respect for him, though I'm not going to read them now. I don't have time, as much as I might like to. The important thing for me now is to get my mind around the Bible—that's the word of God." There's a lot there in the Bible, and it would take a man a long time to assimilate and practice it and to share it with others. That's a lifetime task in itself. I knew that I was just beginning to face up to the difficulties of trying to live and teach the word of God, and I thought that no matter how interesting it would be to read about other religions, I just must keep myself down the straight and narrow road for the time being until I acquired some maturity in the ministry. So I put the gift book on my library shelf and there it remained.

A week or so later I had to go up to another little town to attend the conference of a small congregation. It was a hot summer day when I boarded the big, old, Greyhound-type bus. There were only eight or ten other people on that bus that day, but guess who two of them were? As soon as I saw them I thought, "Oh, no, these are the ones that are going to get me in a corner and let me have it." Sure enough, in just a few minutes here came one of them asking if I'd mind if he shared the seat.

What I didn't realize then was that it wasn't an easy thing for him to do. As it turned out, this young man was at the very end of his mission, having completed his $2\frac{1}{2}$ years there. Now he was on one final assignment, touring the mission to take a new program to the other elders. By the end of the week he would be back in the mission home to be released and then make his way home to be with his family, go back to college, meet a girl, and get married. His temptation now was to ease off the missionary work and just sit back and enjoy this last week in Uruguay.

But now he saw this Protestant minister or missionary, and right away came the old feeling that he ought to go and talk to him. Yet he didn't really want to. But the feeling wouldn't go away. So he asked his companion: "Don't you think we ought to contact that man?" To this his companion replied with a nod of agreement—and promptly turned in his seat to let the other missionary get out into the aisle. To set the example, then, this young man came forward in the bus until he was just behind where I was sitting, and in a soft voice asked me: "Do you mind if I share this seat?"

At first I didn't hear him. (He later told me of this first approach.) Getting no response, he turned to go back, thinking "Well, I tried." But he couldn't go back. He says it was as though his feet were frozen right there and something said to him: "Go back and bear your testimony to that man and tell him what you know is true. That's what you're here for." So he tried again.

This time I heard him and somewhat reluctantly invited him to have a seat. It turned out that we liked each other right away; and we could both sense that neither of us wanted to argue about our religion. Finally, however, we did get around to talking about the gospel, because that was what was most important to both of us. He asked me if I had heard of the Book of Mormon. I told him I had one but that I hadn't read it yet and didn't intend to and then I explained the reason why.

He understood. "Let me show you some of the things that are important to me about the Book of Mormon," he said. None of the things he explained to me then made much impression on me until he began telling me about a promise made by Moroni at the end of the book that if you really want to know the truth of these things, you just ask the Father, in the name of Christ, and the Holy Ghost will let you know. I read that promise and was greatly moved, because I knew enough about the Bible and about God's ways to know that is exactly how he has always worked, and I was amazed that any group of people would put that kind of test on their particular religion or book.

As we talked, I said, "You people rank the Book of Mormon right along with the Bible, don't you?" He answered, "Yes. If that book is false, our whole Church is a hoax." As soon as he said those words, it was as if someone had turned a light on inside my heart. I wanted to read ·the book. I couldn't explain the change. Up to that time I had wanted to put off reading it, but now I had a big thirst; I wanted to read the book.

By now we were nearing our destination. As we were about to part, the elder said that he wished he could talk with me some more about the gospel, but that he was soon to be released and return home, so we probably wouldn't be seeing each other again. At the time this was fine with me, for I wasn't desirous of any more discussions about the Mormon religion. He did say, however, that if there was anything he could do for me he certainly would. So I replied that for my part there was only one thing he could do that might be helpful: he could pray to God that if there was any truth for me in the Book of Mormon I would find it. I really meant this, and he assured me he would pray as I had asked. On that note we parted, he to his church duties and I to mine.

The next morning I returned home before my family was up and made a beeline for the study. Once inside, I closed the door so that Betty wouldn't see what I was going to do. Taking my copy of the Book of Mormon from the shelf where I had stored it, I sat down on a couch by an open window and started to read it. I hadn't the least notion what I was going to find and you can't tell a thing about what is inside by looking at the cover. A man standing on a ball blowing a trumpet is no clue as to what this great book is all about. I figured it was probably about some great old man called Mormon who taught a lot of wonderful things and promised that if you did them you would be a better person and the world would be better off. This is what all the world's religions have—great men who supposedly teach better things than anybody else. You just pay your money and take your choice. I expected that this is what I would run into, so I skipped right over the introduction and began reading what was titled "The First Book of Nephi."

Here I read about a man named Lehi and his sons who left Jerusalem about 600 B.C. at the command of the Lord because the city was going to be destroyed because of its wickedness. It all had a biblical ring to it, and even on the very first page there was mention of King Zedekiah, King of Judah. I saw that and thought: "Wait a minute. He's for real because he's in the Bible. I will go back and check." The Bible is God's record book of all his major dealings with his people. It doesn't have all the details, but the main points he wants us to know are there. So I went back to 2 Kings and 2 Chronicles and found Zedekiah, the last king of Judah. And here come the Babylonians; the city is going to be destroyed, just as the Book of Mormon says. But there's one little detail missing—Lehi. There's no Lehi leaving Jerusalem, nor any such thing. It's just not there; not a shred of it. I looked in the Bible concordance, but no Lehi! What are they trying to prove? I wondered. What's the point of it all? I read on.

Soon it became apparent that whoever wrote this book knew the Bible. In fact, he had even copied a few verses straight out of it, which I thought was only too obvious. Then I began to see what the point was, for when I got over to page 92 I read: "For we labor diligently to write, to persuade our children, and also our brethren, to believe in Christ, and to be reconciled to God. . . . We talk of Christ, we rejoice in Christ, we preach of Christ, we prophesy of Christ. . . ."

Not of Mormon—no mention of Mormon. You have to get to the end of the book to find out who Mormon is. Nothing but Jesus Christ. "And we write according to our prophecies, that our children may know to what source they may look for a remisson of their sins." (2 Nephi 25:23, 26.)

Now, there's no straighter, clearer gospel in the Bible than that. That's the whole point of the Bible—the remission of sins through Jesus Christ. And as I read that, I thought: "This is terrific, even if it is not true. It doesn't matter who wrote it, even if the devil himself wrote it. If a man would take it literally, it would still take him to Christ, and that's right." I didn't know what to make of it. So, I kept on going, and when I came to page 107, the very last words of Nephi, I read this:

"And now, my beloved brethren and also Jew, and all ye ends of the earth [that's me], hearken unto these words and believe in Christ; and if ye believe not in these words believe in Christ."

That is right. That far I could go; but then he said: "And if ye shall believe in Christ ye will believe in these words, for they are the words of Christ, and he hath given them unto me; and they teach all men that they should do good."

And that is true; that is what these words do. You can't argue that they teach anything bad. Nevertheless, to say that they're the words of Christ and "he gave them to me" is the most daring, dangerous, damning kind of a thing to say if it's not true. You just don't serve the cause of Christ in the world by writing fictions about Jesus Christ. I couldn't believe that any honest, responsible group or church or people would put a thing like this across on the world while trying honestly to serve Jesus Christ.

In the next verse the writer of those words goes on to indicate that he understands exactly how serious it is. He says: "And if they are not the words of Christ, judge ye—for Christ will show unto you, with power and great glory, that they are his words, at the last day; and you and I shall stand face to face before his bar; and ye shall know that I have been commanded of him to write these things, notwithstanding my weakness."

That is about the strongest thing I'd ever read in my life, because I knew there was going to be a "last day" before I ever heard of this Book of Mormon. But then in the next verse the writer said the most touching thing I'd ever read: "And I pray the Father in the name of Christ that many of us, if not all, may be saved in his kingdom at the great and last day." (2 Nephi 33:10-11.)

That struck me as wonderful! I thought: "What's wrong with that? That's absolutely right. He doesn't want me to join any "Mormon" Church—no mention of it. Just entrance into the Father's kingdom by believing in Jesus Christ! If that isn't true the Bible's not true either, because that's all that the Bible is about." And yet, if what I had now read was true, why in heaven's name hadn't we heard about it before? I just didn't know what to make of it! I thought: No, it couldn't be true, because for centuries sincere men who loved the Lord and had given their lives for God and his gospel had prayed for more light in the darkness. And they hadn't received a word, so far as I knew—not one word. What I had just read was good, but it couldn't be true because the Father doesn't leave his children in darkness when they ask for light. And yet, if it is not true, what is? If that isn't true, the Bible isn't either. I just couldn't figure it out.

I was getting upset about this whole problem, but by this time my wife was getting upset too! Each morning after breakfast I would disappear into my study and close the door, come out for lunch, then go back in to read, and so on. Betty still fed me, but that was about all. It was terribly hard for her because from her point of view it was ridiculous what I was doing—wasting all day every day for an entire week just reading the Book of Mormon. I ought to be out doing the work of the ministry, calling on people, studying the scriptures, and preparing next Sunday's sermon. From Betty's point of view it all seemed ridiculous. But to me it had become a very serious matter. I had to keep going, even though things were becoming pretty tense in our home.

I read on: King Benjamin, Abinadi, Alma, Helaman, Samuel; wonderful stories that I wanted to believe. Then the thing I had heard about, and kept looking forward to as I read, I finally found in 3 Nephi—the resurrected Jesus came down out of the clouds with the crucifixion wounds in his hands and his feet; the same Lord Jesus healing, teaching, blessing the people. I just wished these wonderful things might be true. There came a sermon on the mount straight out of the book of Matthew, which at first glance seemed too obvious a fraud to be considered seriously. No, I thought again, if Jesus actually did appear and say and do these things, well, that was certainly possible. By the power of God the world was created, and by the power of God Moses crossed the Red Sea; God *could* do these things—that wasn't the issue. The question was, *did* he do these things? That was the point.

So I just put my doubts on the shelf as fast as they came to mind and tried to deal with what the book seemed to say. By the time I had finished reading the book I was really in turmoil about the whole thing. If it were true, I couldn't understand why all this had been kept from the world in general for so long. Yet, if it wasn't true, I didn't know what I believed. I knew that if I went to any of my colleagues in the ministry for counsel, with the best of intentions they could only say one thing. I realized also that if I went to see the Mormon missionaries, they too could say only one thing. But I had to talk to someone outside myself, so I decided to go to the Mormon elders. If this whole business was false, somehow I would be able to detect it; and if it was true, they could help me.

Thus with book in hand I walked over to where the missionaries lived, just a few blocks away, and knocked on the door. I was trembling inside, for I felt like Daniel asking to be led into the lions' den. When one of the missionaries came to the door I said, "I've come to learn." He invited me in, and we sat around in the very humble, simple living room. One of the elders began. "Well, if there was a true church on earth, what would it look like?" I didn't know what he wanted me to say, so he told me that it would have a foundation of apostles, prophets, and so on. Now, I had my own opinions about this. After all, I had never seen any evidence of any true church on earth. They all contained human beings with human weaknesses, so there didn't seem to me to be any point in claiming to be the true or perfect church. In any case, I didn't care to argue the point.

When the elder came to a point where I could break in, I said, "What I really want to know about is the Book of Mormon. What does it mean to you?" He looked me straight in the eye and said: "It's the word of God, and this is the true Church of Jesus Christ, in the name of Jesus Christ, Amen." And then, right in turn, each one of his three companions bore a similar testimony. Completely sincere. But I knew they were sincere before I went there, and I would have been disappointed if they had said anything different from what they did say.

The elder who had been doing most of the talking then asked me if I wanted to be baptized. I replied that I thought perhaps I did when I came in, but I still had some doubts. He then went into his room and returned with a little black book which he said I would enjoy reading when I joined the Church. The book was entitled the Doctrine and Covenants. I had never heard of it. As soon as he had located the page he wanted, he pushed it across the table to me and said: "Wouldn't you like to read this? I think you'll find this helpful." I read out loud: "Hearken and listen to the voice of him who is from all eternity to all eternity, the Great I AM, even Jesus Christ." (D&C 39:1.) This is the beginning of a revelation given through the Prophet Joseph Smith to a man named James Covill, who had been a Baptist minister for about forty years and who had covenanted with the Lord to obey any commandment the Lord would give him through Joseph Smith. The revelation told him to go to Ohio. And the sad, short sequel in the next recorded revelation states that James Covill didn't make it; he didn't keep faith with the Lord. The explanation given is the "fear of persecution and the cares of the world." (D&C 40:2.) The missionaries saw this same struggle going on inside me and felt inspired to share this revelation with me. I was glad to read it, though I didn't know if I believed it. I certainly had never heard of Jesus talking about Ohio, and yet it did sound like the Master! I just didn't know.

Another elder suggested we pray, so we each knelt down at our chairs, the five of us, and took turns praying. I was very grateful for this because it was real and right and I knew what I was doing then. After the prayer we stood up and shook hands, and all I said was that I'd be seeing them. They didn't say anything, but as I walked out of the house I resolved in my heart to fast and pray the next day until I got an answer to my problem.

The next day I went into the little chapel next door to our house, took the Bible and Book of Mormon with me, closed the door, and went up front and knelt down. Then I poured it all out to the Lord—everything that was churning inside me about the mess that I was in now, for I knew what would happen if I went ahead and was baptized. I knew it would be the end of my ministry, but I could take that. I was afraid, however, that it might also be the end of my marriage, for my wife was already extremely upset about what I'd been doing all week long. Furthermore, she had been raised in a Methodist parsonage. Her father at that time was a prominent Methodist minister in the state of Michigan. There just wasn't any way I could explain the whole matter sensibly to her, so I was quite fearful that if I joined the LDS Church I would lose her and the children.

I also worried about my friends, my fellow colleagues in the ministry, and the people who believed in me—those I had preached to Sunday after Sunday for two years in Wisconsin and those I had preached to for the previous two years in Montevideo. They believed that I was preaching them the truth when I said that Jesus Christ is the Savior and the gospel is true and the Bible is God's word. If I went off without any explanation and joined some other church, it would be as much as to say, "Don't believe anything I ever said before." This didn't seem to be the way to build people's faith in Christ.

I poured all this out to the Lord. Then I left it with him and went back and sat down to try to think through things again. I opened up the Book of Mormon and reread the things I had underlined the first time through it to see if they still impressed me now as they did then. They did. I concluded that this book had to be true even though I couldn't explain where it came from and why we hadn't had it before. But then fear would just sweep me off my feet again. "What about your family? Count the cost, realize what you're doing. You've made foolish mistakes in the past." Furthermore, I remembered the counsel of the Lord himself in which he warned that in the last days there would appear groups saying, "Over here is Jesus!" "Beware of such things!" he warned. Yet here were the Mormons saying, "Over here is Christ; he came to these people." They even call themselves "Latter-day Saints"! I just didn't know.

But I did know that Satan is real and that he is working in the world to deceive people. In fact, he had already deceived millions of people in many ways, and could easily have deceived this small group of people called Mormons. And he had deceived me plenty of times in the past, so I knew it could happen again. With this in mind, I would go back up to the altar rail in the front of the empty chapel and pray the whole matter out once again. "Lord, don't let me make another foolish mistake, especially such a big one as this could be!" Then I would return to a seat and go back through the Bible, turning to passages I had grown to love and trust, assurances of God's care and guidance, as well as statements of doctrine about Christ as the Savior and the ministry of the Holy Ghost, and so on.

One such passage that helped me at this time I found in the Gospel of Mark. In talking with Jesus, Peter said: "Lo, we have left all and have followed thee." To this Jesus responded:

> Verily I say unto you, There is no man that hath left house, or brethren, or sisters, or father, or mother, or wife, or children, or lands, for my sake, and the gospel's, but he shall receive an hundredfold now in this time, houses, and brethren, and sisters and mothers, and children, and lands, with persecutions; and in the world to come eternal life. (Mark 10:29-30.)

I read that and thought to myself, "Well, that's the promise of the Lord Jesus; you can either take it or leave it." Then I thought of the time that Jesus had said: "Whosoever shall not receive the kingdom of God as a little child, he shall not enter therein." (Mark 10:15.) And again he had taught that we can trust our Heavenly Father. After all, Jesus reasoned, if one of our own children came asking for bread, we wouldn't give him a stone. "How much more shall your Father which is in heaven give good things to them that ask him?" (Matthew 7:11.)

To me, these and other similar scriptures were all saying, "You *can* trust your Heavenly Father—if you will—but you *must* trust him as his child, or you'll never make it."

Round and round it went like that all day long from about 7:00 A.M. until toward 6:00 P.M. Then suddenly I realized what was happening. Here I was asking God for the answers and was being turned to the scriptures. Comparing the Book of Mormon with the Bible, I concluded that it had to be true even though I couldn't explain it. Then just when I was ready to move out in faith, fear and doubt would sweep over me again and block everything. Finally it dawned upon me that my fears and doubts were not coming from God in answer to my prayers, so I knew where they were coming from.

I put the two books together, walked back over to the elders' quarters and knocked on the door again. This time I said to the elder who opened the door, "I'm ready now. I've got a lot of fears yet, but no more doubts." He invited me in and they all gathered around. One of them had a big grin on his face as he said, "We've been having a great spirit here, fasting and praying for you all day." Of course I didn't know they did that kind of thing and they didn't know what I was doing. But God knew, and together we won.

This all took place on Friday, March 22, 1963. It was now about 7:00 P.M. I thought to myself: "Tomorrow's Saturday. I'll explain to my wife what I've decided to do and try to help her understand. Then Sunday I will tell the people at church what I've decided." I wasn't going to try to convert them (nobody converted me); I'd just tell them that I had found a book that tells about Jesus and I believe it to be true. That much explanation they deserved. Then I would go over to the evening service at the LDS branch where I supposed I'd be baptized.

Just about then, while I was planning this out, one of the elders looked at his watch and remarked that it would take about an hour to fill the baptismal font. That was a sharp curve, but I hung on. "No," I said to myself, "I've fought this thing all day long. There's no more fighting to be done. I've gotten all the answers I need, and all that I'm going to get for now."

So I wandered around town for about an hour in a spirit of prayer and then met the elders over at the lovely new Mormon chapel. We then gathered around the baptismal font, just the four missionaries and myself, and sang in Spanish an LDS hymn, "The Spirit of God Like a Fire Is Burning." I was then taken into the waters and baptized. Moments later we went into chapel, where I was confirmed a member of The Church of Jesus Christ of Latter-day Saints by the elders and received the gift of the Holy Ghost by the laying on of hands. I then went home.

At this point, I of course had not discussed baptism with my wife. I realized later that I ought to have done—that the Church does not recommend that a husband be baptized without his wife's knowledge, the emphasis properly being on converting families. But I am describing the events as they happened.

The next evening, after praying about the matter, I explained to Betty what I had done. She was terribly upset and at first didn't know what we were to do. The next morning she decided we should stay together for the sake of the children until we got back to the United States, where she hoped I would come to my senses. As far as telling the people of the Methodist Church was concerned, I decided to wait a week, and to ask them to be especially prayerful during that week because I would have something very special to share with them the following Sunday. In the meantime, I'd go down to the LDS mission home in the capital city and learn all about the Church (now that I'd joined!), then I'd be in better condition to explain when I came back. Betty was relieved that I wasn't just going to break the news right then, so she went with me down to the mission home, still very upset. She was not at all interested in learning about my new Church, but she felt she should go with me anyway to face squarely what I'd done.

In the mission home we found a sweet family spirit among the many young men and women living there which was wonderful. We were made to feel completely at home; we even ended up doing the dishes. All initiative as to religious discussions was left entirely in the hands of my wife. No one tried to persuade or convince her about anything. With her approval, however, one of the elders was assigned to give us some of the missionary discussions.

After we had been there a few days we were invited to have dinner at the home of President A. Theodore Tuttle, then supervisor of the missions of the Church in South America. After dinner, President Tuttle began to explain very simply and briefly about Joseph Smith, of the time he went into a grove of trees to pray and two Personages appeared to him—one being Jesus Christ and the other, God the Father! They both had a body of flesh and bone. I had never in my life heard such a thing, and it was absolutely thrilling! I knew immediately that it was true, and it swept away a whole fog of confusion about the nature of God. President

Tuttle went on to explain just briefly about when we were all together in heaven before we came down to earth, and it truly seemed as if I could almost remember!

After spending a wonderful week with the "Mormons," we returned to the parsonage, packed up our belongings and flew back to the states. I decided to go to Salt Lake City to live in order to learn more about the Church at first hand. In time I received the true and genuine priesthood of God and learned much of the gospel by activity in the Church. When I received my patriarchal blessing, I was given God's promise in writing that if I were faithful in my callings, I would someday be able to bring my wife into the Church and eventually take her to the temple of the Lord where we would be sealed together in an eternal marriage.

Betty does not follow blindly and she now needed time to accept for herself the story of the restoration of the gospel, so we continued attending our separate churches for over seven years. Then, on a summer vacation trip to see her parents in Detroit, we decided to take in the Hill Cumorah Pageant in New York. Before the show began that evening we took a walk up the hill, and on our way back down I pointed to some kind of concrete structure protruding slightly out of the ground and remarked that that might even be the very box Joseph Smith found the plates in. It was just a casual comment not intended seriously, but it struck her at that moment, and even more forcibly during the showing of scenes from the Book of Mormon, that this really was where the Book of Mormon plates had been buried, and that those stories were indeed historically true. As a result of this experience she opened her mind and heart to the gospel, and shortly after returning to our home in St. Joseph, Missouri, I had the great joy of baptizing her in the Missouri River.

Today our family is united in the gospel, and we can see the gracious hand of our God gently leading us toward the eternal joy he so much wants us to have.

IT PASSED THE TEST

Ritchey Marbury is a true southern gentleman with a mischievous twinkle in his eye. He has acquired many academic and professional honors in his young life. He could also be described as one of the most cautious and conservative investigators of The Church of Jesus Christ of Latter-day Saints. His sincere but thorough tactics of scrutiny are a little amusing as he recounts them, and his account prompts the reflection that the patient Church members who fellowshiped Ritchey and Fonda have earned at least part of their eternal reward by "hanging in" while a fine couple came to the realization that they were converted. That couple love the Church with all their hearts and have become a most active part of it.

Once they accepted baptism, the Marburys progressed remarkably. Ritchey was ordained an elder a month after he was baptized and was called as second counselor in the Georgia District Presidency three months later. He is now president of the Albany Branch, and is in the process of building a chapel to promote the work of the kingdom in south Georgia.

Prior to joining the Church, he once remarked to the mission president that he was used to being active in his church and he was afraid there would not be enough for him to do in the small LDS Church in his area. Somehow this is no longer a concern to him.

My mother and father raised me as a member of the First Methodist Church in Albany, Georgia. I was taught to go to church regularly; to give 10 percent of my income to the Lord because it belonged to him; to pray often; to study the Bible;

and to live as righteous a life as I knew how. I'll have to admit I wasn't a perfect child, but my parents tried, and our family was always very close and loved each other a great deal.

Toward the end of my high school days I was very concerned as to what profession I should choose. (I had actually been employed in my father's engineering firm since I was eleven years old and had gained an appreciation of the engineering business.) I thought very seriously of entering the ministry, for I felt that I ought to be a preacher. To seek the answer, I used the only way I knew—I knelt and prayed about it. My parents had always taught me that prayer was the way to get the answer to anything I needed to know. I've never failed to get an answer, and I didn't expect to fail this time. So I asked my Heavenly Father what I should do—what college I should go to and what should be my life's work. He answered me, but I didn't really understand the answer. First of all, he told me I ought to be a minister, something I guess I had been hoping for. But I got the feeling that he wanted me to go to Georgia Tech. Now, how being a ramblin' wreck from Georgia Tech could qualify me to be a preacher I didn't know, but I nevertheless felt that this was what the Lord wanted me to do. So after I graduated from high school I set out to prepare to be an engineer, a preacher, and a ramblin' wreck.

I've always had a very strong faith in God. I learned that from my parents. And I had enough experience with prayer to know that whatever my Heavenly Father wanted me to do, he'd let me know. I can remember once as a young boy, when my cousin was about to have a baby, the doctors had said that the baby would be deformed. X-rays had been made, and there was no question that one side of the baby was completely undeveloped. I heard about it, and being young and not having any doubts that the Lord would answer my prayers, I got down in my room and prayed to my Heavenly Father that this cousin of mine would have a whole child, one that would not have any abnormalities. After praying, I felt so good about it that I knew the Lord was going to answer that prayer, I knew the baby would be all right. It's a matter of medical history that *that* day, two days before the baby was born, X-rays showed it to be deformed. It's also a matter of medical history that when the baby was born it was completely normal.

While I was at Georgia Tech I met and became very good friends with a boy named Charlie Sellers. Toward the end of the school year our group of friends decided to have a party. I was named as chairman and Charlie Sellers as co-chairman of the party committee. The purpose of the celebration traditionally had been simply to have one big beer blast. I told Charlie he would have to see about buying the beer. I said: "I don't believe in drinking. The strongest thing I drink is Coca-Cola."

Charlie's reply was that the strongest thing he drank was Hawaiian Punch. (I didn't know it then, but Charlie Sellers was a member of The Church of Jesus Christ of Latter-day Saints, and I also didn't know then that Latter-day Saints abstain from alcoholic drinks, coffee, and tea.) We decided that maybe the wrong leaders had been elected for this party. But the more we thought about it, the more we laughed and the more we decided to go ahead and perform the functions we had been asked to perform—and just serve Hawaiian Punch. After all, this would probably be the first party that a lot of these people had attended that they'd be able to go home from stone sober—instead of stoned.

Every time I go back to Tech and see some of my old classmates they reminded me of that party, and some of them have told me they didn't realize how much fun it was to enjoy the night of the party and enjoy the next morning also. In fact, some of them didn't know what was missing until they realized it was the usual hangover.

Charlie Sellers and I became very close friends. We worked together on several projects in school, some of which required us to be out of town overnight. The first night we were in a motel room together, before we retired for the night Charlie suggested that we kneel down and have our prayers. This was his custom. I was delighted and impressed. Later we talked about religions, and he told me that he was a member of The Church of Jesus Christ of Latter-day Saints. I told him that I didn't know any church existed with such a long name. Charlie laughed and told me that they were more commonly known as "Mormons."

Up to that time I had had a great deal of respect for Charlie, but I told him that I knew he couldn't be very good in his Church —that I knew very little about the Mormons, but one thing I did know was that to be a good Mormon you had to have at least four or five wives, and I knew that he wasn't married. Charlie simply smiled and told me that the Church has not practiced plural marriage since 1890; that the Church believes in sustaining the laws of the land; and that all Latter-day Saints refrain from contracting any marriage forbidden by the law of the land.

The friendship between Charlie and myself continued to grow; later he was an usher in my wedding, and I was his best man in a reception celebrating his temple marriage. Charlie told me a great deal about the Church—enough to arouse my curiosity. He told me first that a heavenly messenger had come to this earth and restored all the truths that had been lost since the early days of the original Church. He told me that God the Father and his Son Jesus Christ had appeared to a fourteen-year-old boy named Joseph Smith, and that Joseph Smith had been instructed to organize the Church in the same manner that it was organized in the time of Christ—with apostles, prophets, and all the other offices and appendages of the Church.

Because Charlie was my friend I listened intently, then told him, "Yes, sure, this is possible." All the while I was thinking to myself, "How in the world did I ever get involved with such a screwball as this? This guy's a real weirdo."

Then he invited me to a meeting where there were two young men telling me this same story. They had some little figures on flannelboards. As they told me the story and built up a picture of the Church as it was established, they asked me several questions. They put the figures on the flannelboard, and then after a while they pulled all the figures off, and all the little pieces of flannel fell to the floor, showing how the Church would fall without a foundation of apostles and prophets. I was not favorably impressed with that pair of missionaries, yet something of what they told me stimulated my curiosity. I had obtained a Book of

Mormon from Charlie, and later I obtained a copy of the Doctrine and Covenants and the Pearl of Great Price. I began to read, I began to pray about it, and I began to feel good about the things I read and prayed about.

As I continued to read and pray, I found out that the Church was a lay church. This caused me to wonder if it were possible that, when the Lord told me in the high school period that I should attend Georgia Tech but also that I should be a preacher, he wanted me to go to Georgia Tech to meet Charlie Sellers and hear the gospel. I realized the possibility that if I joined the Mormon Church I would be given something they called the priesthood, in which case I could actually be "a preacher" *and* a civil engineer, and in that way the prayer would be literally fulfilled.

I still had many intriguing unanswered questions about the Mormon Church. I told my wife Fonda, even before we were married, that I was interested in the Mormon Church and that it was possible that someday I might become a Mormon and that she might join with me. At this Fonda laughed more than I had when Charley first told me about the Church.

Fonda and I continued to read a little about the Church, went to LDS meetings occasionally, and met with missionaries from time to time. In 1963 I entered the armed services, being stationed at Fort Belvoir, Virginia, and Fort Knox, Kentucky. During this time we heard that an apostle was going to be at one of the Mormon churches. Fonda and I decided to go and hear him. The first reaction I had when I saw the man was that something must be wrong. First, there was no halo around his head. He looked just like any other man. When he spoke, his voice didn't thunder out; there wasn't a blinding light surrounding his presence. The thing that shook me the most was when I went up to shake his hand and ask him if he knew Charlie Sellers. He said he had never heard of him. "Well," I thought, "What kind of Mormon are you? Any Mormon who *is* a Mormon has got to know Charlie Sellers." I did find out later that Charlie Sellers knew him, and this satisfied me somewhat. Of course I later realized that there are approximately three million members of the Mormon Church, and every member just can't know every other member.

The more I continued to read about The Church of Jesus Christ of Latter-day Saints and the more I prayed about it the closer I was drawn to it. I felt that there was more substance here than anywhere else and I wanted to know more. By then I had heard and read many things pro and con about the Church. I searched for and read everything about it that I could get my hands on, and I was amazed to discover that a great many pieces of literature had been written against the Mormon Church.

By this time we were living in Albany, Georgia, so I decided that if I was going to learn more about the Mormon Church I needed to know something about the members who were living in Albany. One of my wife's piano students turned out to be the daughter of the branch president, Bob Oates. I immediately contacted Charlie Sellers to see if he knew Bob Oates. Charlie knew him, so I knew he was a legitimate Mormon. Now, during my two years in the military I had spent most of the time as an intelligence officer. I had learned how to conduct background investigations on people. I decided to use these skills in finding out all I could about Bob Oates.

One of the first things I did was to go over to his house to borrow a book. I had been reading the Doctrine and Covenants and several pieces of literature about the Mormon Church, which often referred to the *History of the Church*. I decided that if he was a good Mormon Mr. Oates would certainly have a copy of the *History of the Church*. I went over and asked him and he did, so I borrowed it. True to form, several weeks later two young, well-dressed men knocked on my door and said that they were elders from The Church of Jesus Christ of Latter-day Saints. Now, if there was anybody I didn't want to see, it was a bunch of Mormon missionaries. I wanted to study privately about the Church; I was curious, and I guess the Holy Spirit was trying to tell me something, but I wanted to study on my own. I didn't want the help of some people who were already prejudiced about this strange religion. I didn't want somebody who was going to try to convince me to think their way.

Nevertheless I let the missionaries come in, and they said they had a series of discussions they would like to teach me. Not really realizing how dedicated missionaries are, I said: "You know, I'd really like to talk to you, but I'm working on a thesis for my master's degree, so the only time I can talk to you is some time after 9:30 or 10:00 P.M." I knew the elders had to get up between 6:00 and 6:30 every morning, so I figured that this would end the whole thing.

The next evening, right on the nose of 9:30 P.M., there they were. They were smiling brightly and anxious to teach me the gospel. The things they said made sense, and as they continued with the second and third discussion I began to realize that perhaps the things they were telling me were true. We had all but the last discussion; missionaries came and went; and after a while we had heard the first discussion so many times that as they would ask a question and quote scriptures, I'd quote the scriptures. Then they'd ask me if I'd ever heard the discussion before, and I'd tell them, "Yes, this makes about the twelfth or thirteenth time." I'll have to admit they were very polite and very patient, and I wonder sometimes if I'd have the same patience with other people that these great missionaries had with me. I'm so grateful they did.

After Fonda and I had had the discussions, we still weren't convinced we should join the Church. We thought we were perfectly content in the Methodist church we were attending. Our friends were there and we were very happy being socially involved with them. We had between two thousand and three thousand members. The Mormon building was about one-tenth the size and had only a little over three hundred members.

In the Methodist group, at this time I was teaching a Sunday School class on the Old Testament. I found out that at 6:30 every morning the Mormon Church had a seminary class which studied the Old Testament. I was quite eager to learn as much as I could so as to help the class I was teaching, so I asked if it might be possible for me to attend the Mormon seminary.

Actually, I didn't go about it in quite this way. I had been watching Bob Oates now for about six months (I never "bugged" his house or offices), and I hadn't been able to find anything drastically wrong with him. I had come to know that he was dedicated to the Church and to the missionary effort. Now, I didn't want to attend the seminary class very badly, but still I wanted to learn about the Old Testament. I've always had a little bit of mischief in me, and I thought: "I normally get up between 6:00 and 6:30 A.M. anyway, but I bet old Bob doesn't get up that early, and I think it would be funny if I could get him up that early every morning." So I went to see him.

"Bob," I said, "I think I'd like to attend the seminary class that your wife is teaching."

He was delighted. "Fine," he replied.

"But you know, Bob," I continued, "I'd like to have somebody I know go with me, and if you'll attend it every morning with me, I'll go."

Bob said he'd be glad to. He figured that I'd probably go once or twice and that would be the end of it, but what he didn't know was that I was up at that time in the morning anyway, so it wasn't that difficult for me. Poor Bob didn't normally get up until a couple of hours later. As we began to attend seminary, Bob found out that he had a bargain to keep and he was losing quite a bit of sleep doing it. The few mornings that he slept in, I would send a note back to him by his wife. It would always consist of Doctrine and Covenants 88:124, with that portion underlined that says: "Cease to sleep longer than is needful; retire to thy bed early, that ye may not be weary; arise early, that your bodies and your minds may be invigorated."

Bob managed to make it for the rest of that year. The dedication he had for the Church amazed me. He'd already attended seminary as a youth. I'm sure he was attending again primarily to help convert me, and for that I am grateful.

The next year the seminary lessons were on the New Testament. I felt that I had learned so much and grown so much spiritually during the previous year that I again enrolled. As that year ended, I felt very strongly that the Church was true. Yet

I was superintendent of the junior high department at the First Methodist Church at that time, and I still was not dissatisfied with my own church.

There had been a dedication of an LDS chapel in Tallahassee, Florida, during this time, and the Oates family invited me to attend. Elder Harold B. Lee, then a member of the Quorum of the Twelve, was there to dedicate it. I was introduced to him, and I'll always be grateful for the patience and understanding this man showed me and my family. I had many questions and was very sincere, but at the time I was concerned that he might feel I was just trying to be obnoxious. He answered all the questions I asked him, however, and he told me to write to him if I had any more. I wrote him many letters and he answered them. One of his letters was a little over ten pages in length. You can't imagine how humble it made me feel that a man of that position cared enough about some unknown person way down in south Georgia to spend that much time answering a large number of questions that perhaps seemed a little foolish to him. But he realized that the questions weren't foolish to me, and he answered them with all the wisdom and warmth that one would expect to come from an apostle of the Lord. I think those letters had a great deal to do with our eventual conversion.

During the summer, Fonda and I concluded that if we were going to join the Church (we had been studying it for seven years now, and I had studied it quite intensely) we would like to know more about the members. I knew a great deal about the doctrine, but I didn't know as much as I wanted to know about the people. I knew as much as I wanted to know about Bob Oates and everything I found out about him was good, as was true of virtually every other Church member I'd met. But I wanted to see the Church and its people in action in a "Mormon" area.

So Fonda and I took a trip to Salt Lake City. First we wrote to Brother Lee about our intentions, and he graciously arranged for us to meet with a man named Bill Walsh, who would spend a great deal of time with us. Elder Lee also agreed to spend some time with us later discussing questions which might come up during our visit.

When we arrived in Salt Lake we couldn't have been treated more royally. People whom we didn't even know cared for our children. And this man Bill Walsh was like a human dynamo. He took us from one part of the city to the other showing us the sights and made us feel as if we were members of his family. He took us in to see Elder Lee and also Elder Bruce McConkie. We had heard a little about Brother McConkie. When we got in there to see him, the first thing he wanted to know was what was wrong with Glen Rudd, who was the mission president back home. We told him that nothing was wrong with Glen Rudd, that we thought he was a great person. Then he asked, "How long have you known him?" We told him we had known President Rudd about two years, since he had been in the mission. Brother McConkie then asked, in mock surprise, "And you haven't joined the Church yet?" We appeased him with the explanation that we were just a little more hardheaded than most people; and as a matter of fact, we indicated, we had some questions to ask him too.

We told him that we had heard that this was the only true church, and we wanted to know how we could tell that some of the others making the same claim were not true. My wife said: "The Church of Christ says that it is the true church. What about that?" Brother McConkie looked at her with that deep look of his, and then said very quickly and abruptly, "Then you'd better find out—at your peril!" My wife thought she was going to have nightmares for the next few nights, the man scared her so badly. She told me she was convinced that when he said we had better find out, we had better find out.

After the soft and very soothing manner in which Brother Lee had spoken to us, the conference with Brother McConkie was quite a change; a moment that I suppose we will remember for the rest of our lives. It's really amazing the number of great people in the Church, the wide variations in personalities of these different people, and the way each one can affect a person's life for good.

When we returned home from Salt Lake, I was firmly convinced that the thing that my Heavenly Father wanted me to do was to join The Church of Jesus Christ of Latter-day Saints.

Fonda wasn't so sure at the time. As we talked about it and prayed about it, we finally decided that if Charlie Sellers, who was living up in Syracuse, New York, would come down and baptize us (after all, he was the one who had gotten us started on this quest) we would join the Church when he arrived.

Even while we were asking Charlie to come and baptize us, my wife wasn't too sure whether she wanted to be baptized or not. Charlie told us that he was planning upon a vacation to Canada, but that if we wanted baptism he would be honored to come down to South Georgia instead and baptize us. We told him we would call him back and let him know for sure.

Well, we prayed about it and waited about it, and we still didn't make up our minds. Even the day before Charlie was to leave, we still weren't sure. We decided we would like to talk with some other Church members in Albany, so we called Bob Oates. After about a year I had finally decided to quit studying him, and I felt that anybody who could pass the kind of scrutiny I had given him was a man I could talk to confidentially. I don't know why, but I felt he was the type of man who wouldn't mind if I called him up at midnight if I wanted to talk to him about perhaps joining the Church. Sure enough, Bob came over. We talked and prayed, and about 2:00 A.M. I knew that it was the Lord's will that we join the Church.

Now we needed to call Charlie Sellers, who was planning to leave at seven that morning and didn't yet know whether to go north to Canada or south to the southern part of Georgia. I don't know what he did about packing clothes, because I'm quite sure you don't wear the same apparel to Canada that you do when you are going close to the Florida border. At any rate, when we got Charlie on the phone he was of good cheer; in fact, he was delighted to know that we had reached the decision to join the Church. He said he would come right down.

As the days went on, we told the members at First Methodist Church that we would have to resign the positions we had there because we were joining the Mormon Church. We still had no feeling of dissatisfaction with the Methodist Church. But The Church of Jesus Christ of Latter-day Caints would allow us to retain all the truths we had learned as Methodists—the fact that Jesus is the Christ, the value of prayer, the importance of living a good moral life, and so on—and in addition offered continuing revelation as well as explanations, insights and teachings we could get nowhere else.

The more my wife thought about it, the more she wasn't too sure that this was the right decision. She went on a crying spree. When I say this, I don't mean she boo-hooed for one or two minutes. She boo-hooed for days. She wouldn't go out of the house.

Fonda became so upset one day that I went to the bedroom and got down on my knees and prayed to my Heavenly Father. "Father," I told him, "I think my wife is about to crack up. Now, you told us this is what you want us to do, and I know it is right, but Father, can't you help my wife? She is having a hard time. Can't you do something to make her feel better and to comfort her a little bit?"

When I got up from that bedroom floor, I knew things were going to be better. I walked into the kitchen where my wife was standing, still crying, and I told her, "Fonda, I just prayed about you and I know you are going to be all right." I had no sooner gotten the words out of my mouth than the phone rang. I picked it up and the operator said there was a long distance call from New Jersey for Mrs. Fonda Marbury. Fonda immediately tried to regain her composure. Who in the world could be calling us from there? We didn't know anybody in New Jersey.

When Fonda answered the phone, a lady said, "My name is Connie Freeze." (Connie Freeze? We didn't know any Connie Freeze!) The caller continued, "I understand that you are thinking about joining the Mormon Church."

Well, you could have knocked my wife down with a blink of the eye. In the first place, who was this Connie Freeze? and why in the world did she call us? and how did she know that we were thinking about joining the Mormon Church? Connie went on to explain. She said that a fellow named Charlie Sellers had stopped by to attend sacrament meeting that Sunday and he told her he was on the way to baptize a couple who were Methodists.

She told us that she and her husband had been very active Methodists before their conversion. They felt they understood what we were going through and that for some reason or other they needed to call at this time. Now, if that is not an answer to prayer nothing is. Right at the time when my wife needed help the most, someone from New Jersey whom we had never heard of felt the need to call her. Our Heavenly Father certainly hears and answers prayers. Similar situations happen all over the world, I'm sure.

That phone call did my wife a great deal of good. It helped her calm down. We have talked about this many times. I hope some day to meet the Freeze family. They may never know what a great blessing it was when they called us that day, what trial and strain was going on at our house at about that time. But the prayer was answered, Fonda felt better, and later Charlie arrived. Charlie baptized us, Bob Oates confirmed us, and we were now members of The Church of Jesus Christ of Latter-day Saints.

But my wife was still a bit uneasy, not completely converted. She's always been a better person than I, but she wanted to be a little more sure about this decision. (After all, we had only studied the gospel for seven years, and this was a pretty big decision to make after only seven years of study and forty or fifty books!) But she had joined the Church and, like me, she was determined to obey every commandment of God.

Soon our district president moved to another city, and when President Jensen was called to replace him I was asked to serve as second counselor. It was a very humbling experience to be able to serve with such a great man, and I wasn't sure that I was really the one to do it. I hadn't even been to the temple yet and I had only been in the Church four months, but I was assured that this was the job the Lord wanted me to do. I'm certainly grateful for the call. It has put me in contact with many great men who have had a great deal to do with my spiritual growth and my growing testimony.

Since that time, Fonda and I have had the privilege of receiving our patriarchal blessings and of being sealed to each other and to our children for time and all eternity in the Salt

Lake Temple. Elder Harold B. Lee, who had such great patience
with us and such a great deal to do with our eventual conversion
to the Church, performed the ceremony. Charlie Sellers was there
as a witness, with his wife Nellie; Glen Rudd, who was the
mission president when we were first being taught the gospel,
also was a witness; and Bill Walsh, the man who had spent so
much time with us two years before when we had come to Salt
Lake City as nonmembers to learn about this unusual group of
people, was also there with his good wife.

I am grateful for the Church and what it stands for and
for my testimony that its teachings are true. I know that Jesus
is the Christ, that this is his Church restored in its fulness, that
it receives continuing revelation and contains all the gifts and
powers that existed in the original Church. I know that Joseph
Smith was a prophet divinely called to set up the Church in this
last dispensation. I know that the prophet who leads the Church
today is as much a prophet as was Abraham, Isaac, and Jacob of
the Old Testament. I bear this witness in the name of Jesus
Christ. Amen.

Fonda's Story

Finally the day of the Sellers' arrival came—and I waited
for something to happen. I didn't know what, but surely *something* would save me from this fate of being a "Mormon."
Nothing did happen, and on September 3, 1969, reluctantly and
half scared to death, I was baptized into the Church along with
my husband.

It was not the happy day I now know that it should have
been, but at least the deed was done. Heartbroken at having left
the Methodist Church and the many memories it had held for us
since the day of our marriage, I had many questions rushing
through my mind. What would happen to us now? Would we be
rejected by our families and friends? Would my husband still
have a job? (He is an engineering partner with his father, who
is a staunch Methodist.)

After joining The Church of Jesus Christ of Latter-day
Saints, I cried *literally* for four weeks. I really had a case of

homesickness. Nobody knew how I really felt about the Church, and I put on a pretty good front when with the Saints. I had been given a Church job only a few days after my baptism, and I was faithful in attending all the meetings. I was a good Latter-day Saint in that sense of the word, and it was my secret how I really felt about having left the Methodist Church and joined the LDS Church.

But I found that you just can't be with a group of people who are as devoted and sincere as the Latter-day Saints are and not have a little of it rub off. The more I went, the more I could tell what a profound influence the Church had on the members of the branch. I was amazed at the quality of the things we were learning, and I was especially impressed with how much our six-year-old daughter was learning. It was hard to believe how everybody in the Church had an opportunity for practice in public speaking—even the children!

I had a few bad experiences during those early days after baptism. One I will never forget was being called on to speak at the first district conference I ever attended. It was bad enough to be asked to speak without notice (for I have never been a public speaker), but I was asked by the mission president (Glen Rudd) to bear my testimony, of all things! I hardly knew what a testimony was, and I certainly didn't have one! And after that experience I thought I never would have one, for I planned not to attend another conference if this is what happened to people who attended. (Let me say here that while I will never forget that day, I finally did forgive the mission president who called on me to speak. He had every right to expect me to have a testimony. He and his wife are wonderful, gracious people whom my family and I admire very much.)

Several months after we joined the Church I became very ill with lobar pneumonia, and since I was too weak to do anything else I picked up some Church literature and began to read. I think it was then that the truth began to make itself known to me. Sure enough, this Mormon doctrine and these teachings made sense, and everything began to fall into place. I was administered to in the hospital and I could see the surprised look on my doctor's face the next morning when he listened to my lungs. He had done all he could do and was really concerned, since I was allergic to penicillin, which is the primary drug used in treating this illness. I know he was amazed at my sudden improvement, but I knew that it was the hand of the Lord working through the priesthood.

Shortly after I was released from the hospital, Ritchey and I received our patriarchal blessings. In his opening words to me the patriarch rebuked my unbelief. He blessed me to be able to receive the testimonies of others. This has proven to be true. I had closely watched the members of the Albany Branch for so many months as an "outsider"—watched not to observe how they lived up to beliefs they had but to see if they made a slip. Instead of discovering such negative things, I felt their devotion and steadfast love of the gospel touch my spirit. I feel that the way that I was converted into this Church was by becoming a part of it, for apparently that was the only way I could really *know* what the Church is.

I am so thankful now that I was practically "forced" to join the Mormon Church. I needed a little "push," and I am very glad that I had a good-natured husband with a "strong arm."

Today, after three years in the Church, I am amazed at all the Church encompasses. Mormonism is not merely a religion but rather a way of life, and I am very proud to be a part of it. I am thankful that my Heavenly Father saw fit to put me on the earth in this dispensation of time, and I am especially grateful to those faithful Saints who were so loving and patient with me and my family in helping us to see the truth. I know that this is the Lord's Church and the things it teaches are true. I bear this testimony in the name of Jesus Christ. Amen.

John Ritchie

BAPTISM OF A BUSINESSMAN

Consider an active businessman, living and working in the heart of the busy, worldly city of San Francisco, running a Bay Area business; active in civic and business organizations; a man with a lovely wife, four handsome children, and every material possession that modern society can offer. One might think he had everything. Yet he knew that something was missing, even though he could not define that something or how to find it.

Many men of similar background—Ivy League education, material success, influence in affairs—have somewhere had their lives touched by the Church. Some have even been momentarily moved by its message to the point of believing it, yet have not had the courage or faith to pursue this belief to its logical and spiritual conclusions, to dedicate their lives to the building up of the Kingdom. Why did this man?

One of his missionaries, Steven Sorensen, has expressed his appreciation for John Ritchie in these words:

"For one thing, he is sensitive to things of the spirit. Another one of his strong assets was his sincerity, his willingness to conform to the doctrines and requirements of the Church even prior to the time he was taught the principles . . . even though his knowledge of them was little more than hearsay."

This attitude of complete submissiveness to God's will is perhaps the most remarkable attribute of this prominent yet humble and teachable man. Few men of his substance have so willingly answered the call, "Come, follow me."

Not many years ago, The Church of Jesus Christ of Latter-day Saints was an unknown in my life. I had spent my life living as I wanted, doing what I wanted, not concerning myself in any way with "my religion." At the time of my conversion I was privileged to be a trustee-elect of the largest Episcopal cathedral in California, a huge, magnificent church. But I was not really actively involved. Now I am very much involved—in The Church of Jesus Christ of Latter-day Saints. I would like to tell how this came about, with the hope that this story may help someone else.

My conversion came about through some deeply personal experiences—happenings I would now term "spiritual"—which are very difficult to communicate to others, especially in writing. Without pride but in a genuinely humble spirit I attempt to portray them here.

When I decided that I must join the Church I knew very little about it other than the testimony of Joseph Smith. This did not matter, because of the spiritual witness I had received. I can testify that a person's life, his attitudes, his direction, in fact his whole purpose and existence, can be changed by knowing that the Church is true, and by following the promptings given to him, even though he initially knows little about the Church.

1. My Reasons for Joining the Church

In 1968 a very close friend of mine, John Huston, died. Well-known in business circles, he had owned a great deal of property in California and some in Utah. Shortly after his funeral his widow called me: "John, we have a lot of property in Wendover, Utah. I don't know a thing about real estate. Will you go there with me and look at it?" So a couple of weeks later, Pat Huston and I flew to the Salt Lake City Airport, arriving there late one evening. This was my first trip to Utah.

After we had driven to Wendover, it took us most of a day to see the buildings John Huston had owned there. In the late afternoon we hurried back to the Salt Lake Airport in our rented car to catch the plane to San Francisco. As we approached the airport it was just getting dusk, and I could see Salt Lake City ahead of us on the hills. Standing out in the distance was the Temple. I said to Pat, "Let's drive over there. I want to see that building."

The five o'clock traffic was very heavy around Temple Square, people were flocking out of downtown buildings, and finding a place to park was very difficult. By the time we had managed it we had only ten minutes to stay. Pat waited in the parked car while I hurried into the South Gate to see what Temple Square was like. I was very interested in seeing the Temple itself, as I had seen pictures of it in the past and its architecture had always fascinated me. I entered a smaller building on my right, the information building, and spoke to a young man at a counter: "I'm only here for a few minutes. Have you got anything I can read on my way back to San Francisco?" "Oh, yes, take one of these," he replied with a warm smile. So, I put an interesting-looking pamphlet into my pocket, returned to the car, and we drove fast to the airport.

On my trip back to San Francisco I read the pamphlet, "The Testimony of Joseph Smith." It had a very powerful effect on me. I got tears in my eyes as I read it. When I got off the plane I knew that I believed it. I also knew that I had encountered something that would affect my life.

By some blessing for me, that was the right start in my learning about the Church. What better beginning than Joseph Smith's Testimony! I think a convert must read it; he must under-stand and believe it; and he should believe *all* of it. These things I did. Yet for over a year afterwards I chose to put it in the back of mind and continue my very lively life in San Francisco, not concerning myself with Joseph Smith's Testimony or The Church of Jesus Christ of Latter-day Saints.

The following February (1969) some friends of mine said, "John, why don't you go with us this May on a trip up to Ogden, Utah. After a hundred years we're going to drive the golden spike again." These friends made a hobby of collecting old train cars, those built at the turn of the century. We put together a really great train for the occasion. It took about four months to persuade Southern Pacific to let us make the trip, but they finally agreed. Our train rattled from Oakland to Ogden, where we left it at the station while we went to the very interesting centenary ceremony at Promontory Point, an exact re-enactment of the driving of the golden spike in 1869.

By chance, our seats in the bleachers at Promontory were right next to the Tabernacle Choir, one of the greatest missionary aids of the Church. I remembered hearing the Choir in the early thirties on funny-looking radios that are collectors' items today. That sunny afternoon at Promontory Point, as the Choir sang, I was very touched, even though they were singing songs for the occasion and not hymns. My group was having a "good time" drinking beer. I dropped away from them, went out on the sand behind the bleachers, and just lay there and looked up at the clouds and listened. I didn't know it, but something was happening to me up there at Promontory Point, Utah.

The following day we were in Ogden again. I felt compelled to return a second time to Temple Square. I got my wife and son and several of our friends together to go with me to Salt Lake City and we all had lunch at the top of the Hotel Utah. After lunch, we went over to Temple Square. My wife and my son and our other friends went wandering off into the Visitors' Center. I dropped away from them (I didn't know why) and soon found myself standing before an unusual statuary group of three figures —John the Baptist, Joseph Smith, and Oliver Cowdery.

Something spiritual happened to me on that sunny afternoon in front of that statue, though the telling might sound strange except to Church members. There's a tree behind the statue, and suddenly a little wind came up and scattered some of its leaves over me. As I brushed them off, it seemed as though something had touched my shoulder. It was a very distinct feeling. I looked up at the tree behind the statue, and as I did so the sun became intensely bright—so bright that although I was wearing my dark glasses I couldn't look. I knew at that moment that something very significant and personal was happening to me on Temple Square in Salt Lake City.

I stood there in deep reflection, almost as though I were in a kind of trance. I remember that after a few moments a little boy came up and grabbed my hand to ask me a question. I came back to normal consciousness and went into the Visitors' Center to join my jovial friends. There I signed the register.

Later we returned to Ogden, and I rapidly fell back in with our train group and its festivities. On the morning of the following day, on which we were to return to San Francisco, I asked the motel manager (we had transferred from the train to a motel because of the heat) if he knew where there was a certain Trappist monastery in that area. (My brother, who is Catholic, had gone up there many years before on a retreat, so I wanted to see it.) "That's over in Huntsville," the man said. I didn't know anything about the area, but I got my friends together once again and we drove off through a narrow canyon till we finally came to a beautiful valley surrounded by snowy mountains.

I thought I'd seen a lot of beautiful country, but I found out that Utah is gorgeous. We came to some lovely lakes or reservoirs, and we found the Trappist monastery. But it was closed; locked up. As we left its grounds, I noticed a very interesting house on a promontory of land over toward the reservoir. For some reason I felt impelled to drive to that house. I seemed to be drawn to it. I stopped the car and my son and I got out and walked around in front of the house, studying it carefully.

Back in the car, we went on and found a place where one of my friends could buy a beer (that's hard to do up there, but we achieved it), and I asked the man who sold it to him whose house that was and what he knew about it. "Oh," he said, "that's the home of David O. McKay, the President of The Church of Jesus Christ of Latter-day Saints." So there I was in the middle of Utah, looking at the home of David O. McKay. Why was I, who had never been in this region before, drawn to the home of the President of the Church?

Later we traveled toward California on our old train, where I sat with my wife and son on the observation platform watching the tracks recede into the distance. As the sun set, I reflected deeply on the things that had happened to me in Utah. But once again I chose to put the Church into the back of my mind. I was too busy to think about religion; too busy to concern myself with

Joseph Smith's testimony; too busy to consider what was missing in my life.

Because I had signed the register in Temple Square, I soon got several calls from the elders. I didn't know what an elder was, and I laughingly put them off. "Thank you a lot, but I'm just not interested. I would like to meet you, but I don't have the time. I'm too busy right now."

But in February of 1971 my young son Mark, who was attending the Cathedral School in San Francisco, surprised me with an unexpected request. "Daddy, we have to write papers on different religions, and my friend Sam and I are going to write on the Mormon religion. Don't they have a temple around here somewhere?"

"Well," I said reflectively, "yes, it's over in Oakland."

"Will you take me to it?" he asked.

The following Sunday I found myself driving to the Oakland Temple with Mark and his friend Sam Caffrey. I'd seen the Temple many times up on the hill above the MacArthur Freeway, as I'd traveled about the area, but I'd never before been there.

Soon we were sitting by the east fountain in front of the Temple. It was about noon on a very grey, misty Sunday in February. But the Temple is a beautiful place, even on a grey day. I remember remarking to my son at the time (and I then knew nothing about baptism for the dead), "Mark, there's something here that makes me feel the presence of the dead." Soon a friendly man came along and told us that there were Temple tours. We told him why we were there, and he said, "Well, join us at 1:00, and we'll take you through." So we started on the Temple tour.

The first thing shown to us was the movie, "Man's Search for Happiness." It so happens that I have a seventy-five-year-old father who is not well. He has very white, curly hair and a white mustache — a very dignified gentleman, I might say; very handsome. As I watched that movie, onto the screen came the likeness of my own father in the form of the principal actor in that film, with curly white hair and a white mustache. The movie is the story of events in the life of his family at the time of his death, and of his passing into the next life. It struck me right to the heart.

Afterwards we went up on the terrace of the Temple. There is an olive tree at each corner. As I rounded the corner of the Temple with our small group we came to the second olive tree, the one at the northwest corner, overlooking Oakland. With no intent or expectation I dropped away from the group again, just as I had done at Temple Square in Salt Lake City. They went on ahead and disappeared around the corner. Under that olive tree there was a bed of beautiful white pansies. As I stared at this pure white bed of flowers they seemed to move in the wind and then suddenly to become intensely white. I would describe them as becoming as white as snow in winter sunshine, and to this day I cannot forget that brilliant whiteness. I looked up at the bas relief of Christ in the Western World, which is on the wall of the Temple at that spot; and as I did so, despite the greyness of the day, the sun filtered down on that olive tree, exactly where I was standing.

Moments later a flight of birds flew over, and I came out of what again seemed to be like a trance. Again I had a feeling of being touched by something, and I knew very clearly that something spiritual had happened to me a second time. I also knew, precisely at that moment, that it was intended that I should join The Church of Jesus Christ of Latter-day Saints. I stood there for a moment and convinced myself of this truth before moving on to catch up with the tour.

Now I knew that I had received two spiritual promptings intended to direct me to the Church: One at Temple Square before the statue of John the Baptist; the other at The Oakland Temple beneath the bas relief of Christ. Nothing like this had ever occurred previously in my life. It was my decision that, since these happenings were positive and clear and had taken place without prior expectation on my part, I should heed the promptings they gave. Therefore at that moment I concluded to join The Church of Jesus Christ of Latter-day Saints.

At the end of the tour we saw another movie containing some other startling things that reminded me of my own wife and daughter. Maybe others see personal applications in the two films we had now seen, but to me it all seemed to have been planned especially for me that day.

On the following day I contacted Joseph Allen of Utah International, Inc., the only member of the Church I knew well, and told him what I have recorded here. We talked for three hours over lunch, and he advised me as to what I must now do.

That's the first part of my story. There are three parts, and each part is different.

2. Investigation

"Draw near unto me and I will draw near unto you; seek me diligently and ye shall find me; ask, and ye shall receive; knock, and it shall be opened unto you." (D&C 88:63.)

Once I got to the point of deciding to join the Church, I began to get extremely interested in it. Joseph Allen arranged for a bishop to come to my office late on a Friday evening. As a former Episcopalian, I would have expected a bishop almost always to be older, to have a white collar and dark clothes, and to be rather formal. But it was not so with Bishop Dix Newell. He's in his thirties. He was dressed in a business suit such as any businessman might wear. And as he sat with me in our conference room he extended such warmth and friendship to me that I was very touched. It's a meeting I'll never forget. The following Sunday I presented myself at the entrance of the Bay Ward in San Francisco, my first visit to a chapel of The Church of Jesus Christ of Latter-day Saints.

One thing that the investigator discovers early is the simplicity of the services and the simple functional style of LDS ward chapels. I immediately felt at home. After a whole lifetime of elaborate church settings, gone for me were all the old trappings: the great stained-glass windows, the brocade, the hats, the candles, the choir boys, the vergers, the crosiers, the lengthy processions, the cushions, the kneeling at the rail. All of it was gone in a matter of one Sunday morning. Here was simplicity, warmth, genuineness, and love, and I recognized it. I felt strongly as though I had returned to some place I had been to before, and even the friendly faces of many of the members seemed familiar, although I had no consciousness of ever having seen any of them before.

This first visit was a new, strange, and wonderful experience. It was a fast and testimony Sunday, and I'll never forget those testimonies at that first meeting. When he got out on the moon and discovered it was golden and not grey, astronaut Scott said: "Yes, I actually felt at home. I couldn't help thinking to myself, 'Gee, everything's working. Here we are in this beautiful place, and every time we turn around we find something new and exciting.' " That was exactly my feeling when I first became acquainted with The Church of Jesus Christ of Latter-day Saints, and it is still my feeling today. Every time I turn around, I find something new and exciting.

Immediately after that first service I had my first meeting with the missionaries. At that point I didn't know what an elder or a seventy was, and I thought most missionaries were somewhere in Africa! It was Bishop Newell who introduced me to my two missionaries, two seventies he had especially asked to teach me— Steven Sorensen, one of the seven presidents of seventies in the San Francisco Stake, and Drew Peterson. Brother Sorensen said to me, "Brother Ritchie, we'd like to talk to you sometime." I responded, "There's no time like the present." So the missionaries took me into one of the classrooms and we talked for four hours. At the end of that time Brother Peterson asked us to kneel, and he offered a prayer the like of which I'd never heard before in my life. It was a warm and personal prayer. At that moment I felt as though I were already a member. I was not baptized until later, of course, but at that first meeting with the missionaries I felt right away that I was intended for this Church and that it was intended for me.

After that first meeting Brother Sorensen said, "We'd like to come out to your home for a cottage meeting tonight, Brother Ritchie." I smiled as my wife and I waited for them in the living room of our home that evening. Our "cottage" has twenty-two rooms!

I reflect often on the great help and contribution to my life given by my two missionaries. Both were young dental students in San Francisco at the time of my conversion. Steven Sorensen, son of Mr. and Mrs. Wesley A. Sorensen of Salt Lake City, and Andrew (Drew) Wayne Peterson, son of Dr. and Mrs. Wayne Peterson, also of Salt Lake City, were both men of extraordinary dedication to the gospel of Jesus Christ and to the Church. They and their families later became very close friends of my family and me. They have continued their great interest in us from our first meeting. They, their wives and their families are among the best examples of dedicated Church members. I shall always thank the Lord for the influence these missionaries have had upon my life. (As I write this in 1973, I am a stake missionary, and Brother Peterson is my missionary companion.)

My missionaries and I recognized that in the case of a man in middle life, surrounded by the walls of an elaborate business, civic and social structure, and a very complicated family scene, we had quite a job to do. The missionaries were both in their middle twenties. Now, I've dealt with young men in their twenties and thirties for many years, because I employ a number of real estate salesmen, but I've never seen two young men who rolled up their sleeves and went to work on a problem as these two did with me. Of course, we had to do it in our off-work hours— evenings and weekends, whenever we could. I will always consider myself blessed to have had such a fortunate selection of missionaries. We talked, we prayed, we worked and walked together. They explained and analyzed.

For the convert, family involvement and understanding is a very important and sensitive matter. My major dedication and my first objective is the hoped-for conversion of my own family. I pray for this daily. Right now we are a one-member family — I'm the only one in the Church. I am consoled in the realization that many families have been united in membership from a beginning of one plus the help of other Church members.

It makes a tremendous difference if the family makes it easy for the convert. Before the missionaries came to our home I talked to my wife at length. To my mind she's one of the great women of San Francicso — of the world. We have always had a happy, easy life together. When I told her about my feeling for the Church she understood completely; today she understands completely. She's been absolutely wonderful about this, though it has sometimes been very difficult for her. After talking to my wife, I took each of my three teen-age children separately into our library and explained what I was going to do. I telephoned my oldest son in school at Santa Barbara and talked to him for half an hour about it. These conversations confirmed what I knew already—kids are great. They thought it was wonderful. To them, having a Mormon father was and is a fascinating thing. They like it, and they like to talk about it.

So joining the Church wasn't just a new experience for me. It was a new experience for the whole family. As I've come to recognize even more in my own missionary work, those first missionary contacts with the family are so special, so important, so sensitive. Missonaries are seldom working with just one person, for in every household there are many eyes on them, sometimes friendly, sometimes hostile.

I also felt a great need to explain my conversion to my father and mother, Colonel and Mrs. Isaac Haiden Ritchie of San Francisco, both seventy-five. I caught them at the right moment. My father thought it was wonderful. My mother said she would have preferred that I learn to play a good game of bridge! (Recently I asked my mother how she felt about the Church. She answered: "It's made you a much sweeter, gentler, more considerate person, John." I was very touched when she said this.) Several years after this, and shortly after the passing of my father, she attended general conference with me in Salt Lake City.

My wife and I know four or five couples, our friends, that are like family. During my period of investigation I deliberately sought opportunities to be with these friends and explain what I was doing. I had the support and interest of all of them. One of the difficulties in explaining to your friends is that you have to start with the basics, since they initially know nothing of the Church. The big questions were: "Will it change you, John?" "It's bound to change you, John." "Can't you drink any more,

John?" "You can't have any more fun." There was a lot of kidding, and I'm sure some of them thought I must be kidding, too. Of course it was going to change me! It can transform a person's life.

I felt too that I should discuss my change of religion with my salesmen. I run a real estate firm with twenty-eight salesmen in three offices, and we're all very close. It's almost like a fraternity, especially from the looks of their desks! Informally, after a sales meeting at each of my offices, I told them of my decision. Twenty-five thought it was great. Three didn't.

There were others I felt should know, because of my civic and historical work. I'm very close to Mayor Alioto. He seemed to think my joining the Church was a fine thing, and he was quite well-informed about the Church, I thought. I talked to certain members of the San Francisco Planning Commission, on which I serve, and to several officers of the California Historical Society, of which I am the president.

The point is that these are the people I'm close to. I work with them, and they know me well. They know that I'm very consistent in what I do. I've always been in the real estate business, I've always had the same wife, and up to that point I'd always belonged to the same church. To me, joining the Church was and is the major change in my existence; the most important thing I have ever done. I think it's like that to any convert, unless he treats finding the truth more lightly than I think he should.

So right from the start I tried to be very strict with myself in my approach to membership in the Church. I believe that, particularly in middle life, if you join The Church of Jesus Christ of Latter-day Saints you must show your gratitude to your Heavenly Father by making a total commitment, and you'd better be prepared to accept that total commitment. Having lost so many years, having "wandered in the desert" six years longer than the children of Israel, I don't have any time to waste and I want to serve with all my heart, might, mind and strength. I love the Church and enjoy the work.

Another thing I had to do was resign from the Board of Trustees of Grace Cathedral, the cathedral of the diocese of California. It's a great honor to be on the board, and I was a trustee-elect. Steve Sorensen delivered my letter of resignation. The dean of Grace Cathedral told me later: "You could have knocked me over. In comes this young man and says, 'Dean Bartlett, I'm a member of The Church of Jesus Christ of Latter-day Saints, and I have a letter of resignation from your board of trustees from John Ritchie.'" Some time later I asked the dean how he looked upon my conversion. He said: "I was surprised, John, that you would embrace a faith so evangelical in nature and so very contrary to your family heritage."

This resignation was not an easy thing for me. When you've been in one church all your life and when you have memories of many beautiful things there, it's very hard to sever those ties. But in my opinion, after you learn the truth you do have to sever such ties absolutely. You must close the old doors. It is difficult; I've done it, and it's over. Although I severed all other religious affiliations, I have retained memberships, etc., in many organizations, and I know that I am performing a greater service to them than ever. Also, through Church membership my friendships have been broadened and strengthened. Whereas previously I had been in a little tight box surrounded by walls, now these walls are gone and the possibilities are limitless. A few old doors closed, but many more new ones opened.

One of the many things my missionaries did for me, a matter so important for all converts, is to explain prayer as it is practiced in our Church. Our prayers are structured somewhat differently from prayers with which I was previously familiar. On the very first walk I took with my missionaries, they explained the structure of prayer. As a result of learning how to pray sincerely, I have experienced some remarkable, powerful, and uplifting results from prayer. I have had many examples of direct answers to prayer since joining the Church, answers on intimate, personal matters which bear out the Lord's statement: "Therefore, ye must always pray unto the Father in my name; and whatsoever ye shall ask the Father in my name, which is right, believing that ye shall receive, behold it shall be given unto you." (3 Nephi 18:20.)

While I have not achieved it yet, I have hopes for family prayer. I have hopes too for a regular blessing on the food at mealtimes, something I've so far achieved only on occasion.

The missionaries carefully explained to me the absolute necessity for repentance. Every convert has a need for repentance. In my case, after twenty-five years of real estate business and living it up in San Francisco, I had so many spots on me that I felt like a leopard. I wanted to become spotless. The Book of Mormon and the Doctrine and Covenants show that God requires it, but it isn't easy to accomplish. For my final repentance prayer, I went out alone to the San Francisco Stake Welfare Farm, which is a beautiful Christmas-tree farm some twenty-five miles away from my home. I got out in the field on a sunny Saturday afternoon, all by myself, down on my knees, and prayed for three hours. By the time I finished, I knew I was ready to be baptized. I know that repentance must be thoroughly accomplished before baptism, but I am grateful to understand that for wrong done afterwards we can be forgiven through true repentance and through partaking of the sacrament.

As to the Word of Wisdom, upon once learning of its principles I was able to adopt it into my life. Not being a smoker at the time and never having liked the taste of liquor much (although I was most certainly accustomed to drinking as I desired), I had no problem with these two items. Coffee I was most willing to give up; it always had made me nervous. Tea was to me a minor matter. I also found that, through the Word of Wisdom and the guidance of my missionaries, I cleaned up my language, eliminating swear words from my vocabulary.

To me, the Word of Wisdom is primarily a matter of personal discipline. Since I had been raised in a military family, personal discipline seemed second nature to me. For this, and for the benefits of the Word of Wisdom, I am eternally grateful. I know my life will be happier, easier, and longer because of it. Many efforts have been made to get me to violate this principle, temptations open and subtle, but I seem to have gained an inner strength in this regard and have learned the value of a friendly "No, thank you." At first my friends thought I was a kind of curiosity, but after a time they recognized that this was now my way of life.

Early in my Church experience, I saw the need for regular and strict church attendance. I felt the need to partake of the sacrament weekly, as well as for getting acquainted with the members of the Church which attendance brings. It helped me to get accustomed to the atmosphere of the Church. I get a lot of enjoyment out of attending Church conferences too. At the first quarterly stake conference I attended, prior to joining the Church, I was walking down the back hall to look at the first LDS baptismal font I'd ever seen when I bumped into Elder Bernard P. Brockbank. I didn't know what a General Authority was then. Today we write regularly; we've become good friends. Elder Brockbank, once of the busiest men I know, has given of his time for me. His guidance and counsel have been of great help to me and my family as we learn more of the gospel. I am deeply appreciative and thankful for his interest in us.

One day my missionary, Steven Sorensen, asked me to come to his home for breakfast on the morning of a general conference. I'll never forget it. I didn't know what a general conference of the Church was, but I saw it all in color on television. For me, it was out of this world—wisdom, counsel, encouragement from the Lord's chosen servants. And I had my first meal in a Mormon household. It was a big thing for me, a special event. I'd been accepted in that family as a brother.

Another thing I learned to appreciate is what I call the nine basic works of the Church. You normally think of four; I've got nine. After the Testimony of Joseph Smith which I read first, came the three in the Triple Combination—the Book of Mormon, the Doctrine and Covenants, and the Pearl of Great Price (which also contains Joseph Smith's Testimony). I have a leather-bound copy of the Triple Combination presented and inscribed by my two missionaries when I started learning from them. I read every word of it with care (by getting up an hour earlier every morning and going to bed an hour later every night) and had completed it just before I was baptized.

The next two scriptures I read were the Old and New Testaments, from a leather-bound copy of the Holy Bible presented and inscribed by these same two missionaries on baptism day. I read the New Testament for the first time in my life, coupling it with Elder James E. Talmage's *Jesus the Christ.* James E. Talmage is not an easy author to read, but his insights into the life of Jesus Christ make his book a very important supplement to the New Testament. Another great reference work, *Mormon Doctrine* by Bruce McConkie, was given me by my missionaries. I refer to it continually. And for my ninth basic work, for two dollars I bought an LDS hymnal. A book like that for two dollars! Unbelievable! I regard the hymnal as a basic work of the Church. I use it often, even though I don't read music very well. I read it as poetry.

3. *Baptism and After*

I decided that I wanted to return to Temple Square in Salt Lake City to be baptized. My grandfather, a Northwest pioneer and railroad builder, had started out in business in Salt Lake City in 1870. Although not a Church member, he had been a friend of Brigham Young and of other Church leaders in those days. Apart from this, I had developed a special feeling for the song "O Ye Mountains High." At any rate, I felt compelled to return to Salt Lake City to be baptized. This took a little special arranging, but at the appointed time I drove up there with my wife and five children, three of ours and a niece and nephew. It was an enchanted trip.

The day of my baptism, Friday, May 21, 1971, was the most important and extraordinary day of my life. About 8:00 A.M. that morning the telephone rang in our room at the Hotel Utah. It was Elder Bernard Brockbank: "Good morning, Brother Ritchie. Can you and your wife come over to the Church Administration Building? I would like you to meet several of the Brethren." We went right over and were taken into a beautiful conference room where we met and talked with President Harold

B. Lee and President N. Eldon Tanner. What a special and unforgettable experience this was for us! Immediately thereafter Elder Brockbank drove us to Provo, Utah, where we were guests at the ceremonies of laying the cornerstone of the Provo Temple, to be followed by a drive around the BYU campus and then back to Salt Lake City. These events were very special for us, and they are as clear in my memory today as when they happened.

That same evening at six o'clock, as the Nauvoo bell tolled in Temple Square, I was to be there for my baptism. We wondered how we would be received and who would be there, since Elder and Sister Brockbank and my two missionaries were the only people we knew in Salt Lake City. When we arrived there were over thirty people waiting for us, mainly the families and friends of my missionaries. They surrounded us with friendship and love that evening.

Steven Sorensen baptized me. As I stepped out of the waters of baptism I knew I was truly born of the water. My other missionary, Drew Peterson, confirmed me. Eight men came forward for this ordinance. This was a new thing for me, and I'll never forget the feeling of having those sixteen hands pressed on my head. At that time the strength and faith of those men flowed into my body, and through the prayer of Brother Peterson the presence of the Holy Ghost was felt by those in the room. I knew that I had truly received the gift of the Holy Ghost.

Since my baptism, I've become very involved in varied activities in the Church. I have experienced marvelous blessings, among them the privilege of holding the priesthood, working as a San Francisco Stake missionary, and receiving my patriarchal blessing. Truly "my cup runneth over." I have worked with the poor, with the blind, with men in prison. And I have had the privilege of associating with leaders of the Church.

Still I am only at the beginning of the road, and I marvel at the challenges and goals ahead. I know that the Church is true. I know that we are led by a prophet of God. I know that our Redeemer lives. I know that we are the children of the Lord. I am privileged to be a part of Christ's Church.

Having freely received, I must freely give to others so that they might likewise receive. I have written this true account with that in mind. I hope it will help to bring someone, somewhere to accept the gospel of Jesus Christ, that they may receive into their life the great blessings and happiness which that gospel has brought into mine.

PAUL JAMES TOSCANO

A PHOTOGRAPH CHANGES A LIFE

There is more than one way to persuade the nonmember to meet the missionaries of the Church, but they each require that the member exhibit a friendly spirit. Blaine Lee certainly did that. Having made friends with Paul, he asked the "golden question." The response was adequate though not eager.

At the subsequent meeting with the missionaries, the high-school sophomore was at first "difficult." This changed when the missionaries produced a photograph. At that point, so did Paul Toscano's young life. Thereafter his single-minded purpose was to be a member of The Church of Jesus Christ of Latter-day Saints.

His story tells of his frustrating struggle to fulfill this dream, and the stirring testimony of the gospel which all this has brought him.

I was a contentious young investigator. My main object was to show up the missionaries who were trying to teach me the first discussion. I did a very good job of it at first. I argued with them, I challenged their knowledge of the scriptures, and I asked irrelevant questions. I absolutely refused to answer the leading questions they asked me. I hemmed and hawed and hedged. Even when the elders told me the Joseph Smith story, I was unimpressed. I was so concerned about what I was going to say in reply that I didn't listen very carefully and missed the impact of that great message.

Then the missionaries told me about the apostasy, the falling away of the true Church after the death of the original apostles.

This new idea sunk down into my ears and worried me. I made a feeble attempt to defend the succession of Peter down through the line of popes, but I wasn't very convincing.

"Where are the apostles today?" asked the missionaries. "Jesus placed twelve apostles at the head of his true Church. Are they in the Catholic and Protestant churches?"

I was stumped.

One of the missionaries, as I remember, reached into a portfolio or briefcase and pulled out a photograph, a black and white print about 8½ x 11 inches. It was a picture of a group of very dignified men dressed in business suits, some sitting, most standing.

As I looked at it, one of the missionaries explained to me that this was a photograph of the twelve living apostles of the Lord Jesus Christ. When I heard that, I was electrified. For a long time I peered into the faces in the photograph. Somehow I knew that what that missionary had told me was true. I knew by a powerful feeling inside of me that the men in the picture were the twelve apostles of the Lamb. This knowledge changed the course of my entire life.

I was quite a lonely and dejected person; I felt friendless many times, and I ached inside. There didn't seem to be any overarching purpose or reason for my life, and I was very dissatisfied. Then one day, some time in the middle of my sophomore year in high school, a boy walked up to me out of the clear blue and introduced himself. This was Blaine Lee, a fellow student in my Latin class. He'd heard that I played the piano a little and asked whether he could visit my home and listen to me. I was so startled by his request that I didn't know what to say. I wasn't used to such an outgoing attitude, and it made me feel very awkward. I declined his request at first, but he persisted until I finally relented.

When he came to my house I played a few musical selections and then we talked about school. I soon found myself admiring his easy-going attitude. Blaine didn't live far from me, so we would sometimes walk home from school together and have long talks. On one of these occasions the subject of religion came up, and I chattered most of the way home while Blaine just listened to all my strange religious notions. As we neared my house, he interrupted me and asked, "What do you know about the Mormon Church?"

After thinking a minute, I replied that I didn't know much. I'd heard of Brigham Young, but that was all.

"Would you like to know more?"

I said no, and I added that I had a religion and didn't think that I would ever change.

There were a few seconds of silence, and then: "I didn't ask you to change your religion. I just asked if you'd like to know more."

I gave in because I didn't want to hurt his feelings, and he invited me to his house to talk with the missionaries. As I have said, I was contentious at first, but I soon found myself looking at a photo of the twelve apostles; and somehow I knew that they held the keys of the kingdom of God as the missionaries said.

It's been quite a few years since it all happened, but I think I began to get a testimony as I looked at that picture. That's when my life began to change. That evening after I had heard the first discussion, I asked my parents for permission to join the Mormon Church. They adamantly refused to grant it.

Those were very difficult times for me. My parents thought I was merely following an adolescent whim and they didn't want to let me make a decision that I might later regret. On the other hand, I was totally convinced that I had to join the Church. The more I learned, the more I felt that God had called me out of the darkness into the glorious light of his gospel.

For the first time in my life someone had given me concrete answers about God—who he was, what he was like, how I was related to him, and what he had done for me. I began to understand the role of Jesus Christ. For the first time in my life, I learned that the Savior really did save us, that the Redeemer really did redeem us; not from some imaginary danger but from death and hell.

As I studied the gospel, I realized that happiness comes from living the commandments of the Lord exactly. I also began to comprehend the importance of the family unit, my family unit. I knew that for the sake of my parents and my brothers I had to join the Church, even if they frowned on my decision, even if it meant a temporary rupture in the pattern of our lives. I had faith then, and do now, that my family will one day join the Church and be sealed in the Lord's house.

I began to understand these things within weeks of that first meeting with the missionaries, and I soon announced to Blaine that I had decided to join the Mormon Church, a decision I made right after the first discussion. But my parents continued to withhold their permission. I waited for two years. Those were very hard years. There was a great deal of strife in our home, and words were spoken that I wish now had not been said.

There were many arguments, and at times I didn't want to go home at night after school. But somehow I managed to attend my meetings. I remember Christmas of 1962; I was so disheartened that I asked Bishop Jasper Eves of my original ward to give me a special blessing. And with his great heart filled with the Holy Ghost, he laid his hands on my head and in the face of all my difficulties revealed to me that the Lord loved me; and he promised me in the Lord's name that I would soon be baptized into the true Church. With all my soul I prayed that "soon" would not mean another two years.

Three months later, my parents decided that I was truly serious about my decision and that I would be happier if they gave me their permission to join the Church. So they did.

To me this was another miracle and a fulfillment of the promise of the Lord given through my bishop. In the years since then I have drawn much closer to my family. They are not Church members, but we have a great love and respect for one another; and we pray for each other. I am grateful to be the son of my father and mother. I wish now that I could have spared my parents the hardship of those years. I wish I could take back some of the hasty words I said in my youthful frustration. But that is all in the past, and perhaps it was a necessary experience for all of us.

On March 16, 1963, I was baptized, being confirmed a member of the Church the following day. I was eighteen years old and had known the Church was true since I was sixteen.

I realize now one great advantage of being a convert from a non-LDS background. In the years that I've been associated with the Church I can honestly say that I have neither doubted it nor taken it for granted. In my heart I always thank God that he led me by the hand into his true and living Church. Many times, when I am in a congregation of Latter-day Saints, I think to myself: "What am I doing here among these wonderful people? How is it possible that I could be so blessed to be counted worthy to stand among them?"

I have never taken for granted the doctrines of the Church. I enjoyed the years of study I had to pursue in order to make up for the Primary, MIA, Sunday School, and Aaronic Priesthood classes I had missed in my early youth.

But being a convert and the only Church member in a family has some very great disadvantages. A home of divided beliefs exhibits tensions. I have suffered a great deal because of that. Because of my struggle to join the Church and my efforts to adjust to the pattern of Latter-day Saint life, I find that I lack the easy-going, good nature I admire so much in good Mormons from the great families of the Church. There is a blessing that comes with growing up in a faithful Latter-day Saint home. I've watched my Mormon friends, and I've admired that politeness, courtesy, patience, cheerfulness, diligence, obedience, and the gift of soft and easy conversation which come so naturally to them because they learned such habits in their homes.

Many of these qualities were foreign to me, and I had to struggle (and I still struggle) to incorporated them into my life. Too often the signs of the struggle are painfully apparent.

If I had one piece of advice to give to investigators who are seriously considering joining the Church it would be this: Join it, for it is true, the only true and living Church on the face of the earth. But joining the Church does not necessarily mean freedom from struggle, from strife, or from suffering. The impact of such difficulties will vary with individual cases. Some may be required to go through a fiery trial, a purification of their souls, their desires, their motives. But really we should rejoice because in that situation we are not suffering for our sins but are being purified as gold and silver. Peter the apostle declared, "Forasmuch, then, as Christ hath suffered for us in the flesh, arm yourselves likewise with the same mind: for he that hath suffered in the flesh hath ceased from sin; that he no longer should live the rest of his time in the flesh to the lusts of men, but to the will of God." (1 Peter 4:1-2.)

Even if the process of conversion is painful, it is all well worth it. Not all the pain and tribulation in the world can be compared with the glory that shall be revealed in the faithful members of the Church when they meet Christ before the bar of judgment.

I know that Jesus Christ is the Savior of the world. I know that he is the Son of the living God and that he took upon himself a tabernacle of clay and dwelt among men. I know he was tempted and suffered, but that he did not yield to the temptation. I know that he was crucified by wicked men. I know that he visited the spirit world, and opened the gates of the prison.

I know by a power greater than sight that this same Jesus who was crucified was raised again from the dead. And I know that he lives. I know that he appeared to Mary Magdalene, to Peter and James and John and the other apostles and to many of the saints living in those days.

I know that he appeared to people of the Book of Mormon times, and that he taught them the principles of the gospel. I know that in the year 1820 he appeared to Joseph Smith the Prophet and that he has appeared at various times throughout this dispensation of the gospel. I know all this by the power of the Holy Ghost. I yearn with all my heart for the day when my loved ones and I may be permitted to look upon the face of him who is all our joy and our salvation. For in that day we shall no longer be "strangers and pilgrims on the earth" but joint-heirs with Jesus Christ our Master.

KAN WATANABE

JAPANESE BASEBALL FAN REACHES HOME

In leading people to the restored gospel, the Holy Ghost may work upon varied kinds of human traits and interests to set up the initial attraction. Some are attracted directly by a specific doctrine—the nature of God, the apostasy, the Word of Wisdom, etc. Others are drawn in less direct fashion by friendship or admiration for a member of the Church. The youthful Kan Watanabe's initial leanings are traceable to a somewhat more remote source—a love of baseball.

Baseball led via other things to the missionaries. After nearly twenty-five years in the Church, Brother Watanabe can look back on service as (among other callings) missionary, branch president in two branches, elders' quorum president, counselor in the Japan Mission presidency, president of the Japan West Mission, and currently Asian Area Manager of the Translation Services Department of the Church. More importantly, he and his family look forward to a continuing life of service in the kingdom.

———————

Truly the Lord moves in mysterious ways. If I hadn't liked baseball twenty-five years ago, I wouldn't be in the Church today.

I was raised in the countryside by the Japan seacoast in the city of Komatsu, which is famous for its beautiful pottery and fine woven silk. My father was an army officer and later served as city accountant. When I was young, my parents taught me the value of good honest work. In those days, not having any of the modern conveniences, we had to cut firewood for the stoves. There is an old Japanese saying, "Your heart will show in the way you cut the wood." Whenever I would cut the wood crooked, my father would say, "Son you just didn't put your whole heart into it." I can also still remember my mother's having said, "God is with honest people." As I look back on my boyhood days, I often think as Nephi of old must have thought when he wrote, "I Nephi, having been born of goodly parents. . . ." (1 Nephi 1:1.)

During and after World War II, while I was still in my early teens, I attended Komatsu Technical School, where I studied machinery. When I started there, English was a required subject; but by the time I reached my fourth year the requirement to study English had been discontinued.

I have always loved sports, and during that youthful time of my life I was very active in all kinds of ball games—baseball, tennis, table tennis, etc. In front of my home was a ball park where American servicemen (part of the occupation forces) would come and play among themselves or with Japanese teams. I spent a great deal of my time at that park watching the Americans play baseball. I had a friend who could speak English very well; in fact I marveled that he could communicate so well with these servicemen.

One day, something inside me told me that I should study English a little harder. There was no clear reason or purpose in doing so, and at the time I didn't realize the source of these urgings, but as I look back I know that it was the promptings of the Spirit seeking to prepare me for something to come.

Soon after this, two American missionaries from The Church of Jesus Christ of Latter-day Saints came to our school to teach English. They were using English instruction as a proselyting tool then, as the missionaries are now. I heard the announcement that there would be an English class taught by some Americans, and since I had decided to learn English well I attended their class. All I remember about the lesson is that we sang a song, but after the lesson was over I visited with them and then accompanied them on their way home.

In those days the Church was very young in Japan and the Japanese language presented many barriers to the elders. They didn't have as many proselyting tools as they have now. There was no outline of missionary discussions in any form, and about the only translated materials were the Book of Mormon in ancient literary style and a pamphlet called *A Guide to the Mormon Church*. This pamphlet consisted mainly of the Joseph Smith story. The elders gave me the pamphlet and asked me to read it. It described beautifully young Joseph's experience in the sacred grove, and immediately upon reading it I knew it to be true.

It was just as simple as that. I just read the "Testimony of Joseph Smith" and I knew within my heart that it was true. For many years afterward I wondered why this belief came so easily to me. Now I know why. It was the Holy Ghost bearing witness to me of the truthfulness of the things I had read. It was an example of what the Lord said: "My sheep hear my voice. . . ." (John 10:27.)

Naturally, from that time on I started attending the Church meetings. The elders treated me with kindness, and I was greatly impressed by the brotherly love they showed.

Because the Church was so young and as yet there were no local members, there were no sacrament meetings. The elders did hold Sunday School in two cities, however—Komatsu and Daishoji. It took forty-five minutes by train to travel between these two cities, but I attended both meetings regularly and was very active in the Church, though at that time I had not been baptized.

The first assignment I ever had was to give a 2½-minute talk in Sunday School. The assistants to the mission president were to visit the branch, and the missionaries were anxious to make a good impression. They asked me to give a good 2½-minute talk. Unfortunately they didn't make clear the 2½-minute limitation, and I ended up talking for twenty-five minutes about the Joseph Smith story. I was convinced of its truthfulness and had a great desire to share it with others. Even though I was still an investigator, I was given the responsibility of teaching Sunday School.

One day, as I was talking to one of my nonmember friends about the Church, he began to question me. He asked: "In your Church is there some kind of a ceremony you have to go through to be a member?" I replied, "I don't know for sure, but I'll ask the elders." When I saw the elders again I asked them if there was such a ceremony and, if so, what I had to do to receive it. At this the elders explained baptism to me and asked if I would like to receive that ordinance.

In April 1950, at the age of eighteen, I was baptized into the kingdom of God. It was raining that morning as we rode our bicycles toward Tedorigawa, the largest river in Ishikawa Prefecture, but as we approached the chilly waters the clouds parted and the sun came out as though God were smiling down upon us. That day I became the first member of the Church to be baptized in Ishikawa Prefecture.

In reflecting upon my conversion, I can clearly see that the hand of the Lord was there to help and guide me. This help began with parents who taught me true Christian virtues. It continued with a strong interest in sports which led to an interest in English. Eventually this interest in English led me to the missionaries, and from there I was blessed with the witness of the Holy Ghost and a strong testimony of the gospel.

Later on, after serving a mission, I was asked to be a Church translator. I could then see still another reason why the Lord had inspired such a strong interest in English within me. It helped me to fulfill my vocation as manager of the Church Translation Services in Japan, and later, as a mission president, it proved invaluable in working with both American and Japanese missionaries as well as American servicemen in seeking to further the Lord's work in Japan.

Since the first time I read that pamphlet so long ago in Ishikawa Prefecture, I have never doubted the truthfulness of the gospel or the divine origin of The Church of Jesus Christ of Latter-day Saints. I have never doubted the inspired mission of the Prophet Joseph Smith. Most importantly, I have never doubted the divinity of our Lord and Savior Jesus Christ.

Yes, truly the Lord moves in mysterious ways. I praise his holy name.

A TRILOGY OF TRUTHSEEKERS

Three men of great importance to the growth of the Church in Brazil here share their experiences. Their story is actually one great historical event with far-reaching consequences.

Saul Oliveira, Walter Queiroz and Helio Camargo were young Protestant ministers and students at the College of Theology in Sao Paulo, Brazil, the training center for prospective Methodist ministers in Brazil and other South American countries. Each had problems with a few important doctrines of their church.

At that time Latter-day Saint missionaries were circulating in Sao Paulo, and local ministers were being asked questions about the Mormon religion. The idea was conceived of inviting the Mormon leader in Brazil to visit the college and explain his religion. Being unable to go himself on the required date, mission president Asael Sorensen sent his counselor, missionary David E. Richardson in his place, with instructions to present the first three missionary discussions "just as you would to a group of investigators."

David Richardson comments: "When we entered the auditorium our hearts almost failed us, for we saw about fifty ministers waiting eagerly for us. But calling silently upon the Lord once again for inspiration and support, we commenced the discussions, Elder Call writing the notes of the lessons on the blackboard."

As a result of that meeting with those choice LDS missionaries, three ministers resolved their problems. Each has a remarkable story to tell.

HELIO DA ROCHA CAMARGO

I. IN THE FULNESS OF LIGHT

There have been a few examples in scripture in which contact with God has been associated with a great cataclysm, something sudden and violent, like a flash of lightning which tears through the skies unexpectedly. That was the type of conversion experienced by Paul. The religious experience of Joseph Smith was of the same nature. In cases like these the person undergoes a violent shock and, thus overcome, kneels at the feet of the Creator. The spiritual side of life which until then was wandering in darkness is now suddenly illuminated, transformed by the brightness of eternal truth. Thus in a marvelous and rapid manner there is a total transformation of the personality.

Here is a persecutor of the believers who becomes a saint; there is an obscure country boy who becomes a prophet and leader of countless multitudes. There have been many other people, a few of whom have had their experiences recorded, aimless beings lacking spiritual values who through a traumatic conversion grew grace by grace to become numbered among the elect of God.

This was not the case with me. Rather, I would compare my spiritual life with the peaceful spectacle of sunrise, where at first there is no marked distinction between darkness and light. But the darkness constantly recedes while gradually the light grows brighter, making shapes more distinct, colors more vivid, until there shines the full brilliance of the sun, the perfect day.

Since infancy I have felt the presence of God and have sought to draw near to him. As a son in a Protestant home, I learned early in life to love the scriptures and to seek in them the wisdom of the Almighty. The example of my parents, who were dedicated believers, was of great value, and even today the memory of my father is a constant fountain of spiritual inspiration for me.

Educated in the traditions of the Methodist Church, I attended Sunday School from my childhood years, later participating actively in all the various organizations of that church. At twelve years of age, shortly after the passing of my father, I became an official member of the Methodist Church by making the profession of faith.

I never entertained doubts concerning the truthfulness of its doctrines. When eventually a more difficult question would arise, I would reassure myself with the thought that the pastors would certainly be able to clarify everything. I would attribute any difficulty in comprehending certain things to my own lack of knowledge of the doctrine rather than to any real fault in its structure. I thought that when the day came when I could study the gospel more carefully, everything would be made clear to me and the perfect agreement between the Methodist doctrine and the word of God would be proved.

I lived in this faith for many years. Within it, I established my family, and by its principles I tried to regulate my actions. The reading of the Bible, the studying of theological questions, and the history of Christianity always were my favorite subjects. These things were of such great interest to me that I never tired of reading and studying about them; and even though I was constantly involved in the activities of the various organizations of the church, I always wanted to accomplish more and to know more.

As the years passed, this desire became constantly stronger, to the point that I finally made a decision to change completely the course of my life. In spite of being settled with my family and of a life which had been heading in a completely different direction, I enrolled in the College of Theology with the purpose of preparing myself for the Methodist ministry.

One year after enrolling in the college, I was assigned to the ministry of a Methodist church in Sao Paulo, Brazil, at the same time taking classes, as was the custom in the Methodist Church.

One day, during the discharge of these duties, I was contacted by the head of a family who attended the meetings even though he was not an official member of the church. Having been visited by two Mormon missionaries, he invited me to be present at their next visit. I immediately accepted the invitation; but recognizing my complete ignorance of Mormon doctrine, I tried to obtain some literature. With this purpose in mind, I went incognito to the LDS mission home, from which I obtained a copy of the Book of Mormon and one of the *Articles of Faith* (by James E. Talmage), which I proceeded to study. Unfortunately the meeting fell through because for some reason the missionaries did not show up as expected. I therefore decided that the issue was closed, put away the books I had just started to read, and continued my life as a student and pastor.

One of the practices of the college students at that time was occasionally to invite leaders of other religious communities to give lectures. Several representatives of other churches and creeds had already been invited to speak to the students and professors. At that time the Mormon missionaries were very active in Sao Paulo (as they are now) and I thought it would be timely to suggest that they be invited to speak, so that we could evaluate them, what they were preaching, and what they professed, thus placing ourselves in a position to deal with them on the basis of a knowledge of their cause.

After the suggestion was accepted, I was assigned to establish contact with the Mormons. I went back to the LDS mission home, this time carrying an invitation to President Asael Sorensen. I remember counseling him to come personally, fearing that we would waste our time if he sent us young missionaries who certainly would not be in a position to confront such a specialized audience. But the president was unable to come, since he had another appointment (at a district conference). He assured me that he would send competent missionaries in his place.

The young men came on the day designated. Still very young, they impressed us first with their height (six feet four inches).

They were Elder David E. Richardson, second counselor in the mission presidency, and Elder Roger W. Call, who had recently arrived from the United States and at that time knew very little Portuguese.

In the interest of brevity I will just say that the main result of the meeting was the deep impression caused by the testimony of Elder Richardson. The general comment was more or less expressed in these terms: "Everything they preach may be wrong, but the conviction they seem to have is astonishing." Another impressive aspect of the meeting was the courage and calm with which those young men confronted an audience consisting of students, professors, and even doctors of theology who had completed many years of study and held various titles.

In spite of the impression created and the interest these missionaries had provoked, we soon forgot the matter as we went back to our studies and work. Life in the college continued without any changes.

Some time after this event, when the incident had already lost importance in our memories, a new factor arose which, added to the preceding ones, would direct some of us students to new paths. At that time in college we were studying among many others the principle of baptism. The subject took hold of the students, and when the studies and discussions were directed to the subject of infant baptism, which the Methodist Church practices (as do most of the Protestant churches), the students began to ask questions of the professors and to do research in the library. A large group was inclined to see in that ceremony an anti-biblical practice created by the Roman Church in the first centuries of Christianity, and felt that it should be eliminated from the Protestant churches because of its incompatibility with the scriptures.

The discussions increased in intensity, and the more I studied the subject the more convinced I became of the inconsistency of the doctrine. Finally I contacted the authorities of the church and resigned the ministry of the congregation which had been entrusted to me, declaring that I felt it impossible to continue in that position while not convinced on the question of infant baptism.

Meanwhile I continued my studies at the College of Theology, trying to obtain more knowledge which would help me to reestablish faith in that particular principle.

A few days later the dean summoned the four students, three others and myself, who comprised the group that had left the ministry because of doubts concerning the validity of infant baptism. One by one we were interrogated by the professors. Following this interrogation, each one of us received a letter giving us until the end of the quarter to retract our stated opinions. If we did not retract within that time, we would be expelled from the college.

I still have that letter in my possession. It is one of the strangest and most peculiar documents I have ever read—a truly amazing way to cure religious doubts.

Within the designated time period one of the four went back, recanted, and was readmitted. The other two and I, unable to find justification for infant baptism, withdrew completely from the institution and from the Methodist Church.

Being naturally inclined to a religious life, I started to study the doctrines and practices of other churches with redoubled energy and with the intent of finding out which one I should join. I prayed frequently and fervently, asking God to show me the true way not only because of my own spiritual needs but also because of my obligation to direct along the right path the five children God had given me.

I returned to an examination of the LDS books at the same time that I was studying those of other religious sects. By means of prayer and study I began eliminating the various denominations one by one, at the same time directing more and more attention to the doctrines of the Latter-day Saints. Seeking a more direct contact with that Church, I began to attend the meetings at the Sao Paulo Central Branch, even inviting its president, Elder Scott Fisher, to my home where we could discuss some points of doctrine. From these contacts and discussions, as well as from the visits with Elder Richardson and from reading the various books which were lent to me, the truth was gradually becoming obvious and the clarity of the LDS doctrines and their perfect matching with the Bible were becoming apparent.[1]

But with all this I still lacked a testimony. I began to pray more; and I returned to reading the Book of Mormon, always expecting a ray of light to flash through the heavens. One day, however, already tired of so much study and confrontation, I started to make an objective analysis of my religious position: I meticulously weighed every point; I examined the consistency of all the LDS doctrines one with another and all of them with the Bible, and I perceived that there was no need for a violent flash of lightning to illuminate my path. I had waited anxiously for a swift streak of lightning; but I now realized that I had already been walking in the fulness of light for a long time. The knowledge of the truth had not come to me suddenly; it had come gradually in such a gentle and natural way that I had not perceived that it had already been shining upon me for so long.[2]

I kneeled and thanked the Father for revealing his truth to me. I was baptized into the Church in June of 1956, and shortly afterward my wife (Nair) was also baptized. Today by the grace of God we are counted among his Latter-day Saints.

I wish to leave recorded here, together with my testimony, the prayer which I raise to our Heavenly Father that these words might be of benefit for the spiritual progress of those who read them. This I do in the name of Jesus Christ. Amen.

---

[1] Helio studied very carefully, point by point, verifying critical points in his Greek and Hebrew Bibles as well as in his Portuguese Bible. He read books both for and against the Church, but kept an open mind and maintained a sincere desire for truth. Soon after resigning as minister, he began paying tithing to our Church, saying that he knew tithing was a correct principle, taught in the Bible. He had paid tithing to the Methodist Church since he had realized the importance of the principle, but now began paying tithing to The Church of Jesus Christ of Latter-day Saints because it was "closest to the Church that Christ established while he was upon the earth." It is obvious that because he was doing the will of the Lord—attending church, studying, praying, paying tithing, keeping the Word of Wisdom—he was fulfilling and drawing the benefits of the injunction of the Savior: "If any man will do his will, he shall know of the doctrine, whether it be of God, or whether I speak of myself." (John 7:17.)—David E. Richardson.

[2] Helio eventually became a branch president, bishop, stake president, mission counselor, and head of the translation department of the Church in Brazil. During his visit as a bishop to Salt Lake City for general conference, he and his wife Nair were married for time and eternity in the Salt Lake Temple.—David E. Richardson.

SAUL MESSIAS DE OLIVEIRA

II. INTO THE GOSPEL STREAM

I was born at dawn, January 1, in the year 1931 in a small and poor village called Santa Angelica, Brazil.

My mother was a Methodist—very faithful and zealous. I was educated in a very rigorous regime of obedience to the laws of the gospel according to the rituals, traditions and doctrines of the Methodist Church.

My father was a rude man of the backwoods, uneducated and without religion. He brought us great sorrow. Soon my mother became a widow. The strength of a giant was in her skinny body. She alone provided for the family and made it possible to send her four children to school. I remember the nights when my mother sang and read Psalms and taught us to pray.

We survived through great struggles and sufferings. Everything we achieved was through sacrifice.

One day I left the hills and the primitive life of the country to continue my studies in a big city. My mother's desire, her great dream, was that I should become a minister of the gospel. I too felt that I had the talent for that work. I was certain I could do the work of the Lord as a saver of souls. After finishing secondary school I was recommended by the Council of the Methodist Church to enter the Theology College. It seemed like a dream. The poor country boy was now attending college in one of the great cities of the world, Sao Paulo. A fanatic student, I was devouring the books as a starving person would delicious meals.

After a few years of studying, I was designated by the bishop of the Methodist Church to be the assistant minister of a large church. The year after that, I was called to be a minister of a Methodist church in a city next to Sao Paulo. In the second year of my ministry and my fourth year in the College of Theology, something very strange happened in my life. I couldn't understand it.

It was close to midnight and I was still at the college library with three other schoolmates. I was preparing my talk for the Sunday meeting. I glanced through a scripture, one that was very familiar to me. I had almost memorized it, together with many others I had learned in my childhood. But something very strange happened at that moment. The so-familiar scripture was now telling me something different: "Except a man be born of water and of the Spirit, he cannot enter into the kingdom of God." (John 3:5.) I read it many times: "Except a man be born of water and of the Spirit, he cannot enter into the kingdom of God."

My mind was completely disturbed. It was surrounded with darkness, with no way out. How could this be? This scripture was very familiar to me and I had already talked about it so many times. But now it was somehow different, conveying a deeper meaning. My companions left and I was left alone. I went through all of the Bible scriptures on baptism but I was getting more and more confused. Did Christ really say this? Yes, I had no doubt about this. Is baptism essential to salvation? Yes, clearly. Yet multitudes have died without baptism. Was there to be no hope for their salvation? Apparently my church had no answer on this.

I consulted theology experts on this subject, but they were not willing to talk about a matter of such unimportance. They were more concerned about the great theological problems.

I was surprised to discover that, without being influenced by each other, other schoolmates were having similar problems. God was certainly working on many of us. One church practice lacking scriptural support was infant baptism. I made an intense analysis of the doctrine of baptism and arrived at a terrifying conclusion: The whole foundation of a Protestantism of five centuries was being demolished before my eyes. If baptism of children was a farce, where was truth? Surely there could not be a true church on the face of the earth. My dreams were dying, my ideals were disintegrating, my life was empty.

On Sunday a great congregation was looking at me attentively as I stood before them as their minister. I knelt down and sought God's blessing, then I rose and conducted the meeting. I started to talk. I was saying goodbye to the congregation. I could not explain to anybody, even to myself, where I would go. Some people were crying. I too was crying. I was renouncing the ministry and the great ideal nourished during all those years of suffering and struggle. In his own way God was taking me somewhere, I did not know where.

To sing that last hymn was very difficult for me, the last hymn I would sing as a Methodist minister. I can still remember its first words: "Wherever it be with Jesus, I will go. He is my blessed Saviour and King."

I left the ministry having no destination, responding to an irresistible force which was leading my weak and small feet while my eyes strained to see the light of the truth beyond the darkness and shadow.

About this same time, two other Methodist ministers, schoolmates at the college, were leaving the ministry for the same reason. The news struck the Methodist camp as a bomb whose echo was heard throughout the whole church.

That same week, directors and professors of the College of Theology called a meeting. The three of us were going to be questioned concerning our beliefs. The answers could be only yes or no. There was no other alternative, no explanation, no justification. After the meeting I was informed through a letter from the college board of directors that my enrollment was being canceled.

The ministry was my vocation and I could not betray my calling. I was certain that God had taken me from those poor and distant hills in order to practice the ministry. I continued speaking in several churches, trying to find here and there the answers to my prayers. I was confused, but not lost. I was certain that God would give me an answer, or that I was already receiving his answer in this painful way.

One day the thought came to me: "Organize a church . . . yes . . . a church with the whole doctrine of the Son of God would probably be the answer." The idea of organizing a church without being restrained by any religious philosophy, basing it on inspiration from God and the knowledge in his sacred scripture, was heartening to my soul. Perhaps this was the great answer from God.

During that period I spoke a few times with a small group of dissidents from the Presbyterian Church who had organized themselves into a free church. Here was my great opportunity— a church I could imbue with the pure doctrine of the gospel. In a short period of time I became the first pastor of that group. They gave me a house and a reasonable salary. I wrote the constitution of the church. Twelve men were chosen to govern it. I felt happy. It seemed that God had indicated the right path to me. Nevertheless deep in my soul there was still some perturbation.

That church had an eclectic ecclesiology, a little bit of everything. After the first stage, we went to a more important phase of our work: writing a systematic doctrine for the church. It was going to be hard work. Once a week we held doctrinal meetings, and I was left to compose the doctrine. In my task I wasn't tied down to the doctrines of any church, though I would have to satisfy the members of the church, many of whom were old Calvinists of deep-rooted religious convictions. I was free to look for the truth wherever I could find it. I continued my reading and extensive studies. I had at my disposal doctrinal principles of all religions, and I was looking for the truth as a prospector looks for precious stones on the riverbeds among rough and worthless stones.

Among the religious books available, I found several from The Church of Jesus Christ of Latter-day Saints: the Book of Mormon, the Doctrine and Covenants, the Pearl of Great Price, the *Articles of Faith, A Marvelous Work and a Wonder*, pamphlets of all kinds, and many other books such as manuals used by the auxiliary organizations. Among all of these, I remember, there was even a handbook of missionary discussions. As pastor, every week I would teach a doctrine to the congregation, and as I prepared this weekly talk I found there was much more clarity and much greater conformity with the scriptures in the books of the LDS Church than anywhere else. I didn't notice this at first, but as time went on I began to realize that the whole doctrine I was preaching in my church was taken from the Mormon Church.

This worried me. I realized that perhaps I didn't have to write a systematic doctrine; there was one already in existence. From that moment on I devoured all the literature I could find in Portuguese concerning The Church of Jesus Christ of Latter-day Saints. My interest became still greater when I noticed that I was finding the answers on baptism for the living and for the dead, answers to all the doubts that were still attacking my mind. When I learned about the doctrine on priesthood authority I began to see God's answer, his help in my quest for truth. I had been worried about not being able to teach certain doctrines in my church—the doctrine about God, the doctrine of priesthood authority and a few more. I knew that these doctrines as I obtained them from the LDS literature were true, but I couldn't teach them in my church. Therefore that church was not the right way. God was showing me another one.

On the night of December 31, a few minutes before midnight, eleven adults (I didn't baptize children) were before the pulpit ready to receive instructions for baptism. I began to baptize them, one by one. I knew I was wrong. When the last one, a young nurse, came to me to be baptized, my words were pronounced with much difficulty. I could hardly perform that baptism. My hands were trembling, my whole body shook, and the words would almost refuse to come out of my throat.

At that moment I had no doubt. I knew the path I must follow. I could clearly see the answer from God. I called the Church Council to a meeting and told them I must resign. A young Japanese girl, a deaconess, listening to my words, became pale and perplexed at my resolve to leave the church. She said: "I feel as if I am falling into an abyss."

I left that church. (A leader of the Free Presbyterian Church wanted to know more about the reason for my decision. I explained to him in detail the doctrine of The Church of Jesus Christ of Latter-day Saints. Later he was baptized into the Church and became a leader in the true Church.) Not long after praying earnestly to seek the confirmation of my faith and my decision, I called the mission home and asked for the address of the local LDS meetinghouse.

I received lessons from a young missionary, Elder Stevenson. He couldn't speak my language very well, but I was a good investigator. I had already read many times everything available in Portuguese about the Church of Jesus Christ. I had in my hands the missionary discussions, which I studied, so I had no reason to discuss very much with the missionary. The only thing I wanted was to be baptized. He never knew I was studying the lessons in order to answer his questions correctly. I wasn't doing this to please him, but because I had a conviction of the truth.

I was accepted into the Church of Jesus Christ through the waters of baptism on January 24, 1958. God worked slowly in my life, and like a stream that runs through the hills, now peaceful, now turbulent, in my journey I had been constantly seeking the ocean, the ocean of truth, the great ocean of God's kingdom.

Today I have my whole family together in the Church: my faithful and dedicated wife Elvira; my children, Israel, Júnia, Eliana, Eduardo and Dalto. As I look back on my search I see that in the darkness of the past there was an immensity of light from God that illuminated me; and, little by little, my eyes began to see.

Our Heavenly Father has graciously given me many callings within his kingdom: presiding over a branch, serving as a bishop, serving in the district presidency, and lately serving as a stake president and coordinator of the seminary program in Brazil.

God has blessed me and confirmed upon me the talent I had from an early age of preaching the gospel, ministering the word. I know that in his infinite mercy he has called me from the darkness to the Kingdom of Light and has led me with his vigorous and powerful hand so that I could be a member of his true Church, The Church of Jesus Christ of Latter-day Saints.

III. HIS CONSTANT INFLUENCE

I was a student of theology in the Methodist Church and assistant pastor of a congregation in Sao Paulo, Brazil. As in all the other Protestant churches, some of the important things concerning the kingdom of God were not convincingly explained. While studying the scriptures, I felt the need of apostles and prophets in the church, in order for it to be the Church of Christ; I also felt the need for the coming of the prophet Elijah once more to the world, so that God would not smite the earth with a curse as indicated by the prophet Malachi; and even more I felt the lack of applicability to infants of the principle of baptism ("for of such is the kingdom of heaven").

Not being able to continue in the church any longer, I sought some of my teachers to explain my feelings to them. I was shocked at their answers, beliefs and reactions on the matter. Not being able to get satisfactory answers to these doctrinal questions which I thought were important, I sought my immediate superior and told him everything that had been happening, explaining that I could not continue in the church as a member or a student, or especially as a minister.

After this decision I tried to find out from the group of churches I was already acquainted with—Baptists, Presbyterians, Congregationalists, Seventh Day Adventists, etc.—a church which had prophets. I believed that if I could find it, this church would have the answers to the doubts I had as a preacher.

In a short period of time I found three churches which claimed to have prophets, all from the Pentecostal group. I made an appointment with the pastors of each of those churches so that we could exchange some ideas on the doctrines, in the hope of dissipating my doubts. But after these interviews I told each one of them, politely but sincerely, that I knew they were not prophets of God, and that they were mistaken in that claim.

I participated in a meeting of dissident pastors from one of the Congregational churches in the state of Sao Paulo, where I was invited to be one of their ministers. They gave me a book to read and an invitation to attend another meeting with them. We met again a week later, when I presented to them some observations I had made while reading the book.

In the book there was a paragraph which cited a passage from the apostle Paul which reads: "And he gave some, apostles; and some, prophets; and some, evangelists. . . ." (Ephesians 4:11.) I asked, "Where are the apostles?" They answered, "We are." I asked, "Where are the evangelists?" They answered me, "We are." I then asked, "Where are the prophets?" Their leader answered me that prophets were no longer necessary. I then asked them who had said that, to whom it was said, and where it was written; and I added that I would not believe it unless the Lord Jesus Christ had said it. The leader then arose, shook my hand, and said that I did not belong there. I apologized and left, shaking my head, looking for the church that contained prophets.

Very sorrowful, excited and confused, but praying still more to the Lord and studying the Bible more, I continued my search. I always tried to attend a church on Sundays, whichever one I came across, so as not to lose the habit. Meanwhile I talked to several Fathers, Protestant ministers, presidents of spiritual groups, three bishops of the Methodist Church—even voodoo chiefs. I was also dismissed by the secretary of a cardinal of the Catholic Church on the grounds that he did not have time to discuss such matters. During this time, while I received no satisfactory answers, I heard echoes of my doubts from hundreds of other people I questioned on buses, on the streets, and some of the squares in the city of Sao Paulo.

I was called to Rio de Janeiro for an interview with the pastor of a certain Baptist Church I had attended before because of a girl I was dating. This pastor, who knew my situation in relation to the Methodist Church, offered me free studies, besides clothing, shoes, and a church where I could be a clergyman— these things would be mine if I would accept baptism into his church. I replied that my problem was not a question of just joining a church to be a member or a minister but to find the true Church and nothing else, and when I found it I would dedicate myself to it with all my heart, whichever one it might be.

During this period when I was interviewing ordinary people and religious leaders in order to resolve my doubts and find the truth, I went through an unusual religious experience. While most of the leaders were not very worried about the question of baptism of children—whether it should be administered, whether it had any value, taking the view that it made no difference—the members of the several churches still had their own convictions on it without knowing how to manifest them. On one occasion, after I had spent a few hours making a survey in one of the squares in Sao Paulo, I took a trolley to go home. Suddenly, after the vehicle was already in motion, I saw a man in a drunken stupor on the sidewalk. I immediately jumped off the trolley, went over to where he was, woke him up and asked: "Do you think that a child should be baptized?" To my surprise, his answer was different from all of those who preached baptism: *"Baptism is to be given to those who know what they are doing."* Then he leaned his face again on the ground and continued his drunken sleep. What a great lesson!

By now I had become somewhat incredulous and disillusioned and possessed with increasing doubts and fears. Nevertheless I continued praying earnestly to the Lord. One day I was informed by Helio da Rocha Camargo, who was in the same situation that I was concerning the baptism of children, that there was a church in the world that indeed had officials who were called and designated by God, a church with apostles and prophets, and that their first prophet in this last dispensation had accomplished a work similar to that of Moses when he led the exodus to the Promised Land by order of God. Skeptical that such truth could be found in any church, I laughed sarcastically, all the while sincerely wishing that it could be true. My heart beat rapidly. Helio Camargo was a great friend of mine; surely he wouldn't be joking with me on such an important matter!

I went over to talk to the missionaries who were preaching that their church had apostles and prophets. They were missionaries of The Church of Jesus Christ of Latter-day Saints. As agreed upon, without any interruption from me I heard the seven lessons presented by Elder David Richardson, who at the end gave me the opportunity to ask questions. My response was that at that moment I had nothing to ask about what he had said; I would like to know however, what he had to say about the coming of the prophet Elijah. He answered me immediately. I then asked what he had to say about the baptism of children, when baptism should be administered and in what form, by immersion, sprinkling or ablution. I wanted to know who had established for his Church the way baptism should be administered, to whom it had been taught and where it was written. Having listened to the seven lessons, I understood that it was Joseph Smith who had received the revelations. I already knew he was a true prophet. Now the elders had opened their book and were showing me the answer to every question as I was asking it, so I had the opportunity to read it with my own eyes.

I asked for literature. Besides several pamphlets, which I read during that afternoon and from that evening to the next dawn. I also received a Book of Mormon which I read in two weeks. On the days following the visit with the missionaries, I read all I could about Joseph Smith.

Two days after the first meeting with the missionaries we met with them again, this time with Elder Ronald Davey. I asked him to explain the seven lessons again, to summarize them for me, which he did. I asked him to explain them again and again, up to six times, which he did. After that meeting I had no doubt about the Prophet Joseph Smith. I truly knew that he was a prophet of God, and that he had been called of God just as the other prophets had whose histories and deeds we find in the Holy Bible.

We had wonderful meetings at the home of Helio Camargo, where I was then living, and many times we asked difficult questions, trying to argue opposing points of view in order to confuse the elders. After they left, however, we would talk among ourselves and comment that there was really nothing we could say against their answers; we felt that they had completely defeated us.

A few months went by during which we held two or three more meetings with the missionaries, besides making a short visit on Sundays to the Central Branch, Sao Paulo, where we went anxiously to receive teachings.

Even though I knew that the Church was true, that it was the only one with authority to administer the sacraments and at the same time recognizing that the baptisms I had received first as a little child in the Catholic Church and then as an adult in the Methodist Church were valueless and not recognized by God, I was still reluctant to be baptized. I did not want to refuse, and I know that many times I hurt the missionaries with my hard and brusque *no*. I did not want to be opposed to being baptized. I even *wanted* to be baptized, but I was instinctively refusing it. The arguments of the elders were irrefutable, they were clear and even divine; the order of the Master was firm and immutable; but despite all this, I was not ready to decide.

I suggested to Elder Davey that we should pray for a specific period of time and that I had no doubt that God would help me with this problem. We decided to pray for twenty days. I made up a schedule to pray four times a day, that is, every six hours, simply to ask the Lord the same thing. When I went to bed before midnight I set the alarm clock for that time in order to pray and ask God to give me strength to make a decision.

We had only two of the twenty days left, and I was getting impatient; I had been fasting on those last few days. On that night, March 25, 1957, I knelt to pray at 10:40 P.M. and prayed until ten minutes after eleven. I then went to bed. While lying there, I read the Lord's words: *"Ask, and it shall be given you; seek, and ye shall find; knock, and it shall be opened unto you."* Still lying there, I asked the Lord that these words should be fulfilled with me.

I then fell asleep, waking again at five minutes after midnight. In that short period of time I dreamed that I had died right there in the home of Helio Camargo. I was put inside a coffin, and even though I was dead I had the sensation of hearing the buzzing of conversation of those around the table where my body was lying. Soon I felt that my spirit was rising; and I could look down, through the roof, and see my body inside the coffin and the people walking about, some going down the stairs, others going up. I felt that I was rising through layers of clouds, some of them clear and limpid, until I reached a great door which seemed to be made of bronze, very thick and heavy. I reached for the latch and knocked, certain that that was the place I should enter, for that was the door of heaven.

Waiting for someone to answer, I knocked again, when the door started to open and I saw someone dressed in clothes of exceeding whiteness whose whole being was so brilliant that it illuminated a large area around me. I went to this personage, told him my name, and said that I had died and that I wanted to know if I needed to be baptized. The personage replied, "Yes." He talked to me with such authority, with such gentleness, with such love; his words were so penetrating that they seemed to touch my spine and I felt ice cold. The door started to close slowly. I felt myself starting to go down again, and wishing to talk more with the personage. I clung desperately to the frame of the door, using all my strength to attempt to enter and not fall back, not wanting to go down and reenter my mortal body. But my efforts were useless. Down I went, faster and faster, through the many layers of clouds until, through the roof of the house, I was terrified to see my body inside the coffin on the table. Then I felt that I made a great push.

When I awoke I was seated on the bed, tired but in complete peace. A great happiness pervaded my being. I smiled to myself. It seemed as if I was still enveloped in the brightness reflected by the personage who had talked to me. Still seated, I lifted my heart in a prayer of thanks to God for the answer to my prayers.

By morning free of all doubts and fears, sure of myself, in peace, comforted, enlightened, and justified—I informed Brother Camargo that I was going to be baptized. He asked me how I had made the decision. I replied that the Lord Jesus Christ had told me through a dream that I should be baptized. I called Elder Davey immediately, relating to him what had happened and telling him to set a date for the baptism as soon as he wished. I was baptized that same week on March 30, 1957; and on the same day I was confirmed a member of The Church of Jesus Christ of Latter-day Saints and received the gift of the Holy Ghost by the laying on of hands. At that moment, Elder Davey and I received unmistakable signs of the presence of the Holy Ghost.

Today I am very grateful to my Father in heaven and to the missionaries for having conducted me and guided me to the Way, the Truth and the Life, where I have constantly felt the Lord's divine influence.

I know that Jesus Christ lives, that Joseph Smith was a prophet of God, that today we have a living true prophet leading the Church and that we have the true priesthood of God. I bear this witness in the name of Jesus Christ. Amen.

WILBERT EDWARD HUNT

(INDIAN NAME, BLUE SKY EAGLE)

GRATEFUL TO BE A LAMANITE

*In general, American Indians want to know the "truth"
rather than opinions. They get discouraged and impatient with
people who rationalize by saying, "Oh, some people think this
and other people think that." Also, generally speaking, they can
work with untiring energy for the things that they recognize as
needful in their lives, such as food, acceptance, honor, or religious
duties.*

*Throughout his story Wilbert Hunt characterizes these attri-
butes. He and his wife wanted truth and were not confused by
the multiplicity of doctrines around them. When they accepted
the gospel they had hoped for, they also received as a great bonus
the revealed history of their ancient ancestors, the Lamanites.
Now they are unceasingly diligent in the work and exemplary in
the love of the ministry of Christ.*

————————

Nearly four hundred years ago Spanish soldiers and Catholic
priests came into the New Mexico area and conquered my ancestors. Some of my people were forced to be baptized into the
Catholic Church. In spite of punishments and threats, however,
the Pueblo people would not give up their Indian beliefs. Finally
the priests compromised by allowing the Indians to have their
own religious ceremonies after they had attended Mass in the
church. On feast days, after the Mass was over, the statue of
the patron saint was taken into the plaza where the ancient Indian
ceremonies were held, then returned to the church at the end of
the ceremonies. This practice still continues to this day.

My father, who was very anxious to receive an education, went willingly to a mission school in Albuquerque. That was in the year 1879, when he was already eighteen years of age. He was one of the first Acoma Indians to go to school. The only name he had was his Indian name, which the teachers could not spell or pronounce. One day a box of clothing was received from the east, including a suit large enough to fit him. Folded in the suit was a King James Bible with a note in it. The note stated that the donor wanted the boy who could wear the suit to have the Bible and also the donor's name. In the Bible was written the name Rev. Edward Proctor Hunt. This name was accordingly given to my father, and that is how our family has the English name of Hunt.

I was born on the Acoma Pueblo Indian Reservation in New Mexico. Soon after my birth, I was baptized by sprinkling in the Roman Catholic Church, since both my parents were Catholics. Most of my education was received in Catholic mission and government Indian schools. At the Catholic school I attended, all the children were required to learn the catechism. It was hard for me to understand, so it didn't mean much to me as I was very young. When I reached the age of ten, nuns trained me to assist the Catholic priest at Mass as an altar boy. From then on I thought I was a "full-fledged" Catholic, although I did not know much about the teachings of that church. The Mass was always a mystery to me, as I did not understand Latin. When helping the priest with the Mass, I repeated the Latin words that had been taught to me but I did not know what I was saying.

As I grew older my father taught me many beliefs of the Indian religion. These teachings were good and I unconsciously had made them a part of my life.

When I finished school I went to Europe with my parents and a group of other Indians from various tribes. I was surprised to find that the people in Europe were very friendly and that they had a high regard for the American Indians. We made many friends, and this helped me to realize that no matter what nation we belong to we can love and understand each other.

After returning from Europe, I traveled in the eastern United States for twelve years giving educational Indian programs in the schools during the winter months and working with the Boy Scouts of America as Counselor of Indian Lore during the summer months. It was during this period that I began to realize that other religions were good, as well as my Indian religion. I attended several churches with new friends and I was interested to learn some of their doctrines. I became dissatisfied with many of the traditions I had been taught as a Catholic, such as that if I ever left and joined another church, I would be condemned to hell. Such teachings I began to doubt. I found that there are a great many good people in other churches, and I could not believe that just because they were not Catholics they would be condemned to hell.

I felt the need for something, but what it was I could not understand. I thought I might find fulfillment in religion, but the churches I had learned about thus far did not fulfill this need so I was not content with any of them. I found myself continually returning to the teachings of the old Indian religion, but even there I did not find the complete spiritual atmosphere I was looking for.

A profound homesickness came over me, so I returned to New Mexico. It was a joy to be with my parents, brothers, sisters, and friends after such a long separation. My greatest joy, however, was to be with my sweetheart again. She had been waiting for me for a long time. Because she knew I was Catholic, she had been attending and studying the Catholic Church, expecting that she would have to join my church before we could be married. She belonged to the Presbyterian Church, but was willing to change if necessary. Then she found out that my ideas on religion had changed and that it didn't matter to me which church we were married in. In the end we were married in her church.

I soon found out that my wife too was very dissatisfied with her church. We then decided that we should look for a religion that would satisfy both of us. The search began. We prayed about this matter as well as we knew how. We investigated seven churches but were not satisfied with any of them because each was lacking the "spirit" we desired.

We had not found the right church six years later when I was called to serve in the U.S. Army during World War II. I again returned to Europe, this time as a soldier. I prayed all the time I was in the war and I was greatly blessed in coming home to my loved ones unharmed. My only scars were the sorrow I felt at seeing the terrible destruction and killing. I felt that God had preserved my life and brought me safely home for some purpose.

After I got home my wife and I decided not to join any of the churches we had studied but just to live as best we could, helping and taking care of those who needed us. Since we had not been blessed with children of our own, we dedicated ourselves to helping raise our nieces and nephews. We did attend church services on special days like Easter and Christmas.

In 1947 my wife's mother fell and injured her spine. A year later, through the influence of a friend she consented to have the Mormon elders come and administer to her. As a small child I had heard of the Mormons and had thought "Mormon" was a nationality. While in the army, however, on my way home for a short furlough before going overseas, I had had to wait for a plane out of Salt Lake City. On that occasion I visited Temple Square and was very impressed with the beautiful temple and tabernacle. Since I did not go on a guided tour, but just walked around by myself, I did not hear anything about the LDS religion.

When the Mormon elders came to our home to administer to my mother-in-law, they explained about the ordinance of administration. I was very impressed when they asked for her full name, as the medicine men in my tribe, when praying for the sick, always asked for the full name and clan of the sick person. In the prayer these were used, even as the elders used the full name when administering. This made me think that they might have what we were looking for. When the elders asked if they could come back and teach us the gospel lessons, we all gave our consent.

As the elders taught us, I continually compared their teachings with the Indian religion. Because of my knowledge of the religious beliefs of my tribe, many things they taught I already knew and believed.

Here are a few comparisons:

1. Preexistence. All my life, when anyone died, I heard my people say, "They have gone back to the Great Spirit." I reasoned that a person could not go back if he had not been there before.

2. Life after death. The spirit had to be *alive* to go back to the Great Spirit.

3. We are all brothers and sisters. In my tribe we always addressed one another as brother or sister, even if we were not related.

4. We have a mother in heaven. Since all living things have a mother, my people believed that we had a mother in heaven.

5. The welfare program. Many years ago my tribe had what they called the "chief's field." All the men and boys helped with the farming of this field. The food that was harvested from it was stored in the chief's storehouse. During the winter, if any family ran out of food they were supplied from the storehouse. This arrangement is similar to the bishop's storehouse in The Church of Jesus Christ of Latter-day Saints.

When we started to read the Book of Mormon, it was a great joy to me to learn the correct name of the American Indians. I knew that the name we went by was given to us because Columbus thought he had landed in India.

Through prayer and an earnest desire to know the truth, I received the manifestation of the Spirit that The Church of Jesus Christ of Latter-day Saints is the true restored Church. I knew that it had all the teachings that my Lamanite people had once but had since forgotten. I knew that the only salvation of the Lamanite people was in this Church and that they could not be lifted up in any other way but through the gospel of Jesus Christ. This is expressed in several Book of Mormon passages, for example:

"Yea, I say unto you, that in the latter times the promises of the Lord have been extended to our brethren, the Lamanites; and notwithstanding the many afflictions which they shall have, and notwithstanding they shall be driven to and fro upon the face of the earth, and be hunted, and shall be smitten and scattered abroad, having no place for refuge, the Lord shall be merciful unto them.

And this is according to the prophecy, that they shall be brought to the true knowledge, which is the knowledge of their Redeemer, and their great and true shepherd, and be numbered among his sheep.

(Helaman 15:12-13.)

On September 12, 1948, my wife, mother-in-law, two nieces and I were baptized. This was the beginning of a new life for us. The blessings we began to receive filled our lives to overflowing. Soon more of our relatives were baptized.

Not long after we joined the Church it became necessary to build an addition to our church building. My nephew and I were assigned to dig the new baptismal font with picks and shovels. We both felt very humble and as we dug, with tears running down our cheeks, we prayed that we would baptize many of our Lamanite brothers and sisters in the font. Needless to say, these prayers have been answered. Many Lamanites have been baptized in that font—some by us and many by the missionaries.

When my mother (who could not speak or understand English) was eighty-two years old, she requested baptism. I was interpreter for the missionaries as they taught her the lessons. After the lesson on baptism, she stood up and bore her testimony that she knew these teachings were true and from God. She then asked me if I had the authority to baptize her. How humble and grateful I was to be able to tell her, "Yes, Mother, I have the authority of the priesthood, and I can baptize you." I felt that if my father could have heard the lessons he too would have accepted the gospel. (My wife and I have done the work in the temple for my parents and have had them sealed to each other.)

In 1952, there occurred two of the most important events in our lives. My wife and I were then sealed for time and eternity in the Salt Lake Temple. In that same year we were set apart as missionaries to "forever" teach the gospel to the Lamanites. We have been on two stake missions and are now on a part-time Arts and Crafts Mission under the social services department of the

Church. I am teaching twenty-five Lamanites the art of silver-smithing, or making Indian jewelry.[1]

In 1953 I was set apart to be the first president of the Albuquerque Lamanite Branch, and I served in that capacity for six years. Later I was ordained a high priest and served for one year on the high council in the Albuquerque Stake of Zion. I tell this humbly, as it is a testimony to me that when we do the Lord's work we grow in the Church.

In recent years I have been fortunate to return to Europe several times with my brother, Wolf Robe. Five years ago I went to Israel. I cannot explain the humble feeling I had to walk on the same ground that Jesus walked on and to see the places he had been to. I felt so thankful to be a member of his Church.

In closing, I want to testify that I know that Jesus is the Christ and that he lives; that The Church of Jesus Christ of Latter-day Saints is his restored Church; that the Book of Mormon is true and contains the recorded history and religion of my ancestors; that Joseph Smith was a prophet of God and that all the presidents of the Church have been prophets of God. I know that there is no true happiness on earth except to live God's commandments and to do his work. I am grateful to be a Lamanite and grateful that I was born here in America, the land "choice above all other lands." I bear this witness humbly in the name of Jesus Christ, our Lord and Savior. Amen.

---

[1]"From Joseph Smith to the present time, our Church leaders have manifested a sustained interest in the Indian people and a desire to assist the Indian people to reclaim their heritage. The great thrust at first was missionary work followed by teaching the Indian people skills and occupations that would help them improve their standard of living. The Church now has a very extensive educational program and placement program and a program of social services and health services to help the Indians raise themselves with dignity to a better life."—Dale Tingey, Director, Institute of American Indian Services, Brigham Young University.

JOHN G. KINNEAR

CONQUERED BY LOVE

Meaning, purpose, direction—none of these found place in the young life of John Kinnear. Dimly sensing these needs yet powerless to supply them, he was caught up in the social round, the "rugged" life of the Rhodesian male which encouraged sensual satisfactions but discountenanced any expression of the finer emotions. How could those emotions be appealed to to lift John to the gospel environment?

The Lord found a way. Brother Kinnear now looks back with gratitude on his conversion, his emigration to the United States, his temple marriage, his years as a seminary teacher, his service with the Improvement Era, *his ordination as a seventy, and his privilege of serving on two stake missions, among other Church callings. He will be eternally grateful to those missionaries who brought him into the Church "by gentleness, kindness, patience, and love unfeigned."*

———————————

The little former British colony Rhodesia (then Southern Rhodesia), was officially opened for LDS missionary work, by missionaries in the South African Mission, in September 1950, after a short, abortive attempt at commencing the work of the Lord in that country in 1937. I was baptized in Bulawayo on December 22, 1952, in the shallow end of the city's olympic-size swimming pool. It was then 6:00 A.M., and the daily trickle of early-morning swimming enthusiasts would not begin until 7:00. That day, at twenty-two years of age, I became (I believe) the first Rhodesian-born adult male to accept the gospel.

On that day of baptism, I left behind me a contemporary but almost Alma-the-Younger background—a world filled with fast motorcycles, fast-living people, and an inbred philosophy of "When you're dead you're a long time dead, so live life to the full while you've got it"; a world where liquor bills often exceeded food bills; a world where the Rhodesian male was considered somewhat less than masculine if he couldn't take his booze, tobacco, and women in easy stride; a world where the display of natural affection, even by father for son, was considered a show of weakness. The word that seemed to be uppermost in the Rhodesian male's vocabulary was "ruggedness."

As a boy, I can remember lying in bed at night pondering the subject of death. The thought of a complete discontinuance of life beyond the grave seemed pointless and I abhorred it. I would literally cry out in disbelief and confusion at the thought that the grave was an end to all existence. Why was I here? There seemed to be no point to life. I grew up accepting the "eat, drink and be merry, for tomorrow we die" philosophy, yet deep inside something prevented me from believing in that philosophy literally and following it assiduously. My older sister Dorothy, the girl who was to exert the strongest possible influence on my young life, had inscribed Shakespeare's immortal words in a cherished autograph album:

> This above all,—to thine own self be true;
> And it must follow, as the night the day,
> Thou canst not then be false to any man.

At least I had that to hold on to while I set out on my tempestuous and rudderless journey through the sea of life. Like thousands of young people, I was in a search to find myself, but I was without compass or sextant and could not even determine my current location.

Life seemed futile, yet deep down, despite my many faults and failings, there were some strange limitations as to what my conscience would permit. Even as a boy, I was never able to lie effectively, and blatant dishonesty was distasteful to me. I learned at a very tender age that stealing a candy bar from a store left me with such feelings of guilt that I resolved that my laissez-faire philosophy would exclude this and similar forms of vice.

Throughout my school days, I was exposed to the Bible as part of the curriculum of the (all-male) schools I attended. I am deeply grateful for a foundation of Christian learning. I was a nominal Presbyterian. In high school, my headmaster (principal), a Presbyterian, often personally supervised the religious instruction of the Presbyterians. The whole school assembled for devotional every morning, chanted the Lord's Prayer together, sang a hymn, and received instructions for the day from the headmaster. Each class period found the class in question "toeing the line" before entering the classroom. We stood silent, toes on a painted line in the corridor, waiting for the arrival of the black-robed teacher. "Lead on!" he would bark, and the class would file into the room, each boy standing beside an appointed desk. "Seats!" he would command, and we would sit in unison. No boy asked a question without raising his hand and receiving the teacher's acknowledgement. We stood to phrase the question and sat before receiving the reply.

I came under the eagle eye of the headmaster on more than one occasion but felt the sting of his cane for an infraction of rules only once. I was behind a bicycle shed fraternizing with older boys who were smoking cigarettes, a habit that no high school boy was permitted to indulge in. I quickly deferred taking up this "adult and sophisticated" pastime until after graduation. I never mentioned to my father that I had been caned. Such a revelation would have only brought about additional punishment at home.

As to the extent of my religious instruction, I learned about Christ's life and received some basic instruction in Christian values. The actual nature of God and his relationship to Christ, however, remained one of those never-discussed subjects that one was left to ponder about if he so desired. Either no one thought about it or, if they did, they didn't dare ask for enlightenment. In the rush and excitement of growing up, few of the boys worried about it. For me, however, death remained a part of the mystery, and existence seemed meaningless.

In my home we did not broach the subject of religion, and

church attendance was seldom a family affair, though we all went to church on special occasions like weddings and christenings. All such events were invariably followed by a party at which a fair amount of alcohol was consumed. I had acquired a taste for spirits at a very early age; and, as I grew up, liquor became a social necessity, a way to loose inhibitions and cover up feelings of inadequacy and inferiority, an effective means of buoying up a sagging spirit, and a marvelous escape from the challenge to face problems squarely. It helped solve the ache and meaningless- ness of life.

My school days were extremely well disciplined. Each day began with an assembly of several hundred fourteen- to eighteen- year-old boys, dressed exactly alike in smart school uniforms. Exactly alike that is, except for the "perfects" (appointed student- body officers) whose dark blue ties carried two thin stripes instead of one. I eventually had the privilege of wearing two stripes and becoming the "head perfect." Graduation was an escape from purgatory, a release from discipline and arrival at freedom!

From eighteen to twenty-one I had four years of what I thought was absolute freedom. I now know that absolute freedom is absolute frustration!

I studied correspondence courses for a year but really didn't know what I wanted to do. I acquired a job as a junior map compiler and draftsman for the Surveyor General, bought a motorcycle, changed jobs four times, went to every picnic and party I was invited to, camped out frequently in the magnificent wild Rhodesian bush country, indulged myself in whatever activity pleased my fancy, became engaged to a young lady from England, and interlaced all after-office-hours activities with liquor.

Turning twenty-one is probably the most eventful day in the life of a Rhodesian and involves an elaborate "coming out" party and being given a "key to the door"—a symbol of complete freedom from parental and other supervision. Sobriety is not the common denominator of this gala event. At twenty-one I was still without real direction—still being driven and tossed.

That year my sister Dorothy, who was now married and living in a small town called Umtali, wrote to my parents suggesting that I might be interested in meeting some Mormon young men who had become acquainted with her and her husband after tracting her apartment house. I'm sure she could see the need for reformation in my life and sensed that the elders might bring it about. I told my Mother to tell her to stop trying to interfere in my life, a practice I felt she had conscientiously followed from my babyhood, but which had instilled in me some manners basic to being a gentlemen. Dorothy's next letter announced that she had asked the elders in Umtali to have the elders in Salisbury contact me. I was chagrined by the vision of intense, preachy people with beady eyes spouting hellfire and brimstone doctrines and pointing out what little hope I had for reaching a vaguely defined and seemingly unattainable estate called "salvation."

My father, mother and I discussed at length the impending visitation of the Mormon preachers. My father was a former regimental sergeant major. With strong military phrasing, he indicated his displeasure at the thought of having an evening of religion in our home. Although he had departed Scotland at seventeen and had never returned, he could recall rumors that some of the prettiest Scots girls had been wafted away, cloak-and-dagger style, to Salt Lake City by Mormon elders. Also my mother, who was born in South Africa of English parents, remembered that as a girl, during the Boer War period, she had been told to keep off the streets at night because "the Mormons will get you!" As for me, up to this time the word *Mormon* had not been a part of my vocabulary. I persuaded my father that I could hardly have these "men of the cloth" visit me alone over a beer at some local pub. Since my sister had been born on my father's birthday and my father held a special affection for her, I was quick to point out that she was the cause of the predicament. He agreed that the elders could come to the house but quickly added that he would not be around to hear their message when they came.

It seemed that I was doomed to face the discomfort alone. But instead of coming to my home, the elders sought me out at my place of employment, my cousin's jewelry shop. That was my first encounter with real live Americans and also my first meeting with Mormons—Elders Gary Whiting of Mapleton, Utah, and Mead Squire of Manti, Utah. When one of them asked the manager for me and pronounced my name in a way I had never heard before (Kee-nar instead of Kin-near), I must admit I thought to myself, "Oh, oh! Here are the Mormons." But to my great surprise, they were neither preachy nor did either one have beady eyes. Elder Squire was a very tall former BYU basketball player, while Elder Whiting was a rugged, freckled-faced former BYU football player.

The elders asked if I were the one with a sister in Umtali. I said yes. They asked if I would be interested in listening to their message. I told them no. I hastened, only in the interest of good manners, to add, "You are welcome to come to our home and tell us a little of what you believe, but I am really not a religious person." Like admitting a vacuum cleaner salesman, I thought one visit would be sufficient to satisfy any obligation I might have to my sister. "Listen to their story, hear their pitch, and your duty will be done. You don't have to buy a thing," I told myself. "You will be off the hook, and the matter will die a natural death."

The elders came, they saw, they conquered. Never before had I met young men with any sense of deep belief and conviction about anything. They related the story of Joseph Smith with complete sincerity. "They actually believe this," I thought. (The strange story of the appearance of God and Christ to the young American, however, was no more strange than the parting of the Red Sea by Moses or the miracle of the burning bush ascribed to by Presbyterians!) I admit I thought that the idea of God appearing in America seemed, at first, to be the height of presumption. America had everything. Now they had God appearing over there. "Really, what nerve!" I thought. I have since come to fully appreciate the reasons and significance of this American manifestation and gospel restoration—where else, indeed, could the development of a "revolutionary new religion" have taken place?

At the end of that first evening with the elders, they asked if we might unite in prayer. There was no prayer or blessing on the food in our home; no discussion of religion. We were all embarrassed by the request, and I had a momentary feeling that we might then embark on a sea of religious frenzy. But the prayer was sincere and direct. There were no pious cultivated tones implying, "We are the elect of God; and you, you poor souls, are doomed to the deepest recesses of hell." There was only courtesy, consideration, acceptance, and love.

So powerful was the effect and spirit of the missionaries that they had my non-church-attending, militaristic and frighteningly remote father reading from the Bible—all this in a home where religion had little or no root. I was amazed at these very unusual young men. What was the source of their inner strength and conviction?

The missionaries, may the Lord bless them, persisted. On one occasion I told Elder Squire, "You are not going to make a convert out of me." He replied with typical Mormon diplomacy: "As long as you listen to our side of the story, Brother John, that is all we ask."

It took the best part of a year before I decided upon baptism. I read the Book of Mormon and, though I gained very little from it upon the first reading, I realized that here was a volume that was indeed the word of God as revealed through prophets on the American continent. I have since learned to love the great men of the Book of Mormon—the young, enthusiastic men like Nephi and General Moroni and the older men like Abinadi and Lehi. Most of all, I love Alma the Younger. He was once, in the words of the Book of Mormon, among "the very vilest of sinners." What true greatness he attained through the change in his life!

Joining the Church was not a light or easy decision for me. My older brother wanted to know if I was becoming a Mormon or a moron. My fiancee returned my ring fourteen days after my baptism. My mother felt, at first, that I was too young to throw away my life and become "religious." "Enjoy life," she told me. "When you're older, there's time enough to be religious." My father remained silent on the subject. Only one of the friends from my school days tried to understand what I was trying to do. Others shook their heads in disbelief, firm in the conviction that the conversion would be a temporary thing and that I would return to my old sinning self in short order. My sister, though she never joined the Church and never accepted the gospel, counseled me not to be concerned about what others think. "Don't even worry about what Mum and Dad think," she said. "Don't worry about what even *I* think. You do what you believe to be right. You only have to answer to yourself and to God for what you do." With that sage advice from one whose life is bonded to mine, I was baptized.

Now I wanted to follow in all respects the straight and narrow path so newly revealed to me, but I had a deep sense of inferiority. How could I be sure that, with my irreligious background, I would measure up? In terms of righteousness I could not touch the feet of some of these fine young men who had taught me and showed me who I was, where I came from, and where I had the potential of going. But I could and did promise, "Father, I will strive to do all I can to always measure up." I am still bound by that promise. And in more than twenty years of Church membership, the Lord has blessed my life beyond my ability to comprehend, while refining it with tests and trials and opportunities that have made my testimony stronger.

The Mormon missionaries brought meaning into my life and gave me the answers to those questions that had haunted me since boyhood. I now knew that I existed before I came to earth in the form in which I now exist and as I will exist beyond the grave; that earth life is not a meaningless interlude between nothing and nothing but a purposeful period of character growth and progress toward eternal life. I had learned that, despite the vicissitudes of life, there is a Heavenly Father who loves us and who has provided for our true happiness through a meaningful and logical plan of salvation; that none of his rules or commandments are restrictive, all being designed through the infinite capacity of his love to elevate us to be fellow citizens with the Saints and true sons and daughters of God. I now knew for certain that Christ is the Son of God, and that his life and mission was a significant and vital part of the plan of salvation; that God again reveals his will through prophets as he did in biblical and Book of Mormon times; that "men *are* that they might have joy," "the glory of God *is* intelligence," "as man is, God once was, and as God is, man may become." And I realized that the influence of the Holy Spirit is a real, discernible force.

I moved to the United States almost a year after my baptism to attend Brigham Young University, get an education, and try to make something useful out of my life. I met a "native" Utah girl who almost looked like a double of the girl I had been engaged to in Rhodesia. I had thought about returning to Rhodesia following my degree, but she changed those plans. We married in the Salt Lake Temple in 1956, following my tour of duty in the U.S. Army. We now have five "Afro-American" children around whom our lives revolve and who have added the cement to what we hope will be an eternal family relationship.

In the years I have lived in the United States, I have had blessings too numerous to relate in this narrative, some of them being too sacred and personal for publication. I know that the priesthood is the literal power to act in God's name; I have experienced its healing power and I have witnessed its miraculous influence. I have many times experienced the guiding and protective hand of the Lord in my life and have come to realize that he must have a great love and concern for me. Many times I have been given not that which I have wanted but that which I can see, in retrospect, has been good for me and conducive to my development.

I have been fortunate enough to enjoy the love of a wonderful American foster family who sponsored me when I came to the United States. I was, at that time, a very insecure young man. Jeannie Wilson, mother of one of the South African missionaries during my period of conversion, has been an especially strong influence in my life and epitomizes the love and generosity of the Saints. When I was on my way to the United States, Sister Wilson was fifty-two and the mother of seven children. When asked at Relief Society, "Jeannie, how many children do you have?" she quickly responded, "Seven, and one on the way!" I was, indeed, the one on the way, and every member of that wonderful family has never stopped making me feel as much at home as if I were indeed a member of the immediate family.

The Church gave me an appreciation for my own father, a man for whom I had little affection or understanding until after baptism. My sister used to tell me he was not the hard man his exterior seemed to show. I didn't believe it until the experience I had with him shortly before departing Africa for the United States. It was then that my father, in a rare breach of a communication barrier, asked, "John, are you going overboard for this 'Mormonism' racket?"

"Dad," I replied, "I wouldn't try to fool myself. I believe it with all of my heart, and I'm going to try to live it as best I can."

He responded with a look directly into my eyes that I will never forget. "I know. And just remember, wherever you go, you are still my son."

A shocking thing then occurred. He did something that no one in our family had seen him do and that no self-respecting military man would be caught dead doing—he embraced me and wept. My mother, who observed the scene, later told me, "In all the years I've been married to him, I have never seen him shed a tear."

I learned to love my father in the brief twenty-minute span I spent with him before the fireplace in our Rhodesian home. If I could thank the Church for nothing else, I would thank it for helping me to learn to love my father; to appreciate him for all the fine qualities he possessed. My father drank to excess, but he was an honest man. He only feared revealing those inner emotions that in his world could leave a man naked on the threshing floor of life. I know that I could not love him more were he a stake president. If I had to choose my parents or my place of birth all over again, I would make no changes.

Throughout my years of Church membership, I have never looked back; and my testimony of the truthfulness of the gospel, though put to the test on several occasions, has remained strong and intact. I have come a long way from the first meeting with Mormon elders in Rhodesia, in terms not only of distance travelled but of personal development. I still have a long way to go. How grateful I am to missionaries who believed in me at a time in my life at which I was rudderless and without belief in myself. They gave me direction, spelled out the purpose of existence, and gave me the compass of the gospel, by which my subsequent life has been given real meaning. Had they been less patient or persistent, I shudder to think of what my life would have become. I was brought into the Church by gentleness, kindness, patience, and love unfeigned. I pray that I may be given the ability to affect the lives of others in the same way.

WILLIAM ROBERTS

THE LAST HOUSE

With World War II over, William Roberts returned to his home in New Zealand after several years' absence abroad on active service. Reunited, he and his wife took up again the business of living.

Being together again was wonderful, but after a while not enough for complete happiness. Though pleasant and carefree on the surface, life surrounded thoughtful people with doubts and questions, particularly as the effects of the war took their toll. Too many of life's questions seemed to defy solution.

In his brief but fascinating account we learn how William and his wife met the gospel. He accepted baptism "provided that I am never asked to do anything in the Church." The recollection of these "famous last words" must sometimes provoke a reflective smile from William Roberts, Regional Representative of the Twelve for New Zealand.

In the early fifties in the land of New Zealand, as with many other nations, we were emerging from the effects of the Second World War. In our country we were still struggling for rehabilitation, seeking to overcome the shortages caused by the greatly reduced national manpower. Returned servicemen individually and their immediate loved ones who had courageously kept things going at home—all had to make tremendous adjustments.

My wife and I had been married four years when war broke out in 1939. Following voluntary military training I enlisted in the army, where I was to spend five years which included over four years' service in the North African desert and the Middle East theatre of war.

Meantime back in New Zealand my wife served as a company secretary, taking over a man's position. During those long weary years of war, she and I built up emotional fortifications while we yearned for the end of it all and for our reunion which would follow. Only wonderful comradeship in the armed forces made these years bearable for me.

In 1945 I finally returned home to my dear wife, whose hair, a soft brown before the war, had now turned to grey. Her complexion, however, was still fair—all roses and cream. We became involved in the post-war society—superficially lighthearted but still unsettled deep down as a result of the doubts and questions raised by the war and its aftermath. Life standards seemed to be diminishing. My wife, who has always been an uncomplicated, lovely person, sought particularly to find the truths of life by daily study of the Bible.

Her Bible searchings had been going on for some time when one day our friends gave us a warning—Mormon missionaries were in the neighborhood, and we would be well advised not to open our doors to them. Soon after this, my wife happened to be standing in the front bedroom looking out across our beautiful tree-lined avenue when she saw two young men talking to each other. After what seemed to be a lengthy discussion, they crossed the road and knocked on our front door.

This took place during working hours, and I of course was at the office. My wife let the young men in immediately, realizing that they must be the missionaries about whom the neighborhood was giving warning. She had never heard of Mormonism, but she was very interested in the missionaries' message. Almost immediately she recognized the ring of truth in what they had to say and began to find the answers to many of her questions. Especially she was interested in what they explained about Ezekiel 37—the sticks of Judah and of Joseph.

Soon the missionaries were making evening calls each week. Rather reluctantly at first, I became involved in these evening discussions. These young men always seemed to help me find an answer to my own questions. After a while I knew that my wife was converted, and she joined the persuasive young men in their efforts to help me see the light. They came to dinner once a week, and over the dishes we continued our discussions. After a few months I became softened by the Spirit to the point where I could recognize the truth.

This was a great change to make, a change from the old rough life of my experience into a life subject to the gentle influence of the gospel. Nevertheless I asked for baptism—"provided," I added, "that I am never asked to do anything in the Church." So at six o'clock on a beautiful Saturday morning, March 8, 1952, my wife and I were baptized in the Auckland harbor.

I am sure my wife did not have to make nearly as many adjustments as I had to. I was previously a smoker, but have never smoked since my baptism. Joining the Church changed my life in many ways. My wife and I suffered casualties among our many friends because of our membership in the Church—we were regarded almost as traitors to the cause of society and became the subject of adverse discussion among many groups we had known.

I guess our conversion would be quite commonplace in the history of missionary work if it were not for one factor. When the two missionaries were debating with each other on the other side of the street opposite our home, they were trying to decide whether or not it was worth while knocking upon the door of our house—the last untracted house in the whole of the North Shore district of Auckland. Of the many thousands of homes in this district, not one home had yielded to the missionaries' quest; not one kindly, interested soul had been found. After this experience they were almost entitled to think that they should catch the next bus and ferry back to the city of Auckland. This was the subject of their debate. Because they resolved this question in our favor, we became the first converts to be baptized on the "Shore."

If they had not crossed the road to visit our home and thereby completed their assignment 100 percent, my wife and I may not have experienced the marvelous blessings that have been continually poured out upon us and our family ever since. It almost frightens me to think that my life may never have been changed: that I may never have been sealed for time and all eternity to my steadfast and lovely companion; that we may never have had such wonderful sons—raised in the Church, successful in serving outstanding missions in Canada and Japan, educated in the way of the gospel, married to choice young companions in the temple of the Lord; that we may never have had the opportunity to guide still another young man toward his missionary goal; that we may never have had the privilege of meeting so many wonderful Saints, including our great Polynesian people, whose sole purpose seems to have been to make our lives completely happy and purposeful; that we may never have met living prophets; that we may never have prospered materially, and particularly in truth and light and in peace; that we may never have known the true meaning of love and its eternal nature.

All these exhilarating and marvelous experiences may not have entered our lives, had not two missionaries decided to complete their assignment. With each new day I thank our Heavenly Father for those conscientious young men and for inspiring them to bring the glorious gospel message to the "last house."

GARY GILLUM

GUIDANCE ALONG THE WAY

"With my whole heart I have sought thee: O let me not wander from thy commandments." (Psalm 119:10.)

Sometimes life brings occurrences which are beyond human explanation. Nor could any human being produce the same effect with any known power.

Such occurrences we call miracles.

Miracles have been a feature of the true Church whenever it has been on the earth. Church members do not boast of them; but they do acknowledge the hand of God and bear record of his marvelous dealings with his children in this day as in past ages.

Such a record is this account, delicately told by Gary Gillum, who prepared for seven years for the Lutheran ministry before finding the restored gospel of Jesus Christ.

Relatives of such converts naturally desire that their loved ones serve God and their fellowman. They have reason to rejoice. As Brother Gillum now knows, there are no greater opportunities to serve than those enjoyed by members of The Church of Jesus Christ of Latter-day Saints.

———————

The eastern skies of the Oklahoma panhandle were crimson-orange as the sun rose one January morning in 1963. It was still dark enough to use our headlights as we sped along the new highway. Suddenly another pair of lights approached us in our lane.

After I had regained consciousness a few minutes later, I found myself in a strange world—one of peaceful serenity.

My entire body felt numb. Since I was in deep shock I could move none of my limbs to know how badly I had been hurt, but the shouts of people around the car made me realize our serious predicament. Nevertheless I remained wonderfully calm, as if a loving Heavenly Father were sitting next to me.

When I found myself in Guymon Memorial Hospital I was so thankful to God for sparing my life that I felt no pain when I should have, and even when my heart stopped beating for a few minutes I was conscious and remembered everything that happened. Other extraordinary things occurred. I was expected to come down with fatal pneumonia because of the condition of my lungs, yet I experienced little discomfort. My doctor also informed me that I might be paralyzed from the waist down for the rest of my life; yet after lying on my back for ten weeks I could immediately walk across the room with little assistance. Five facial bones had been broken, but all of them healed without noticeable scars. Later my doctor told some visiting surgeons that I had experienced the most miraculous recovery he had ever witnessed during his entire medical career.

Unknown to me at the time, the Lord must have been preparing me for something. As I look back at those ten years, none of the physical miracles were really as astounding as some of the dreams I had when I was so close to passing through the veil. At the time I experienced the dreams, they kept my spirits higher than they had been even before the accident, but I was at a loss when attempting to interpret those beautiful dreams. It was miraculous that, even though I had not been furnished with an interpretation of those dreams, I was nevertheless able to feel the spirit of them, for they gave me undreamed-of anticipation for things I expected to be fulfilled in my future.

The interpretation began eight years later almost to the day. That day was the exciting and inspiring occasion when I was sealed to my dear wife in the Manti Temple in January of 1971. As Lyn and I drove to Manti at five in the morning, we could see the temple as far as seventeen miles down the road. What a remarkable resemblance between that scene and one in my dreams! In the temple itself those dreams or visions became clearer, but not until after successive visits to the temples of the Lord did I obtain a fuller understanding of them. They had been visions of activities I had never before heard of or witnessed; but I had previewed them—six years before I had joined the Church! The buildings in the vision were unusual also, for they were LDS temples, and the activities therein were Latter-day Saints performing work for the dead.

The events surrounding the accident were indeed God's answer to my prayers. Even though I was listed as critical for almost a week, the Lord did not let me die. I feel that he wanted to give me an experience which I would remember for the rest of my life.

Two months before this accident I had experienced various periods of depression, mostly revolving around uncertainty about life itself, my goals, and my friends. I had yearned and prayed for escape from the responsibilities of life, but my mother had indelibly imbedded the concept of faith in my heart so that I knew that all would work together for good "to them who are the called according to his purpose." (Romans 8:28.) I had had a premonition that something was about to happen; and I had even considered leaving a note for my roommate before departing for home at Christmas, thanking him for all his help and encouragement.

I am not sure what had caused such a conflict in my emotional, psychological, and spiritual development. I do know that I experienced uncertainty concerning God, I felt loneliness, and I took part in the struggle to be an individual—these were the problems which, despite its positive aspects, crept into my adolescent, searching life. During my junior high school years in Albuquerque, Pastor Carl Hiller was a tremendous influence on my life. Very few sermons do I remember as well as his homily on the New Testament passage, "Feed my lambs." Its good influence began to change my vocational goals from that of an airplane pilot or an aeronautical engineer to something more lofty and idealistic—I began to be motivated more by a desire to do some good for humanity than by a desire for personal success.

My family moved to Fort Worth, Texas, and it was not long before my parents had invited two seminary choristers to stay in our home during their tour. They made a great impact on my spiritual life and my budding thoughts toward study for the Lutheran ministry. My parents and grandparents had always kept God and the church foremost in their lives and, as their offspring, I caught the significance of the joy of Christian living. I also became acquainted with Pastor Dorre and Vicar Lange, both of whom were added catalysts to my desire to serve the Lord. I next came under the influence of Pastor Edwin Pieplow, a giant among Lutheran ministers. Through his very example as well as by his meaningful discourses he provided the stimuli which pushed me over into the realm of a final decision. His active influence remained for several years, culminating in a delightfully spiritual summer when I served under him as a summer vicar.

Spiritual leavening and influence caused my dedication to rise as I went on to junior college in Winfield, Kansas. The President of St. John's, Reuben Beisel, was a good friend and confidant in my spiritual trials and questionings. Professor Harold Buls (that wonderful, short, pacing, Greek teacher of mine) was a kindred spirit if ever there was one, leading me down the revealing paths of ancient scripture into the more unmolested, untranslated originals. He alone remains the only non-Mormon who ever bore his testimony to me that God lives and that Christ was his Son.

Music provided an outlet for my avocational and extracurricular activities, and David Krause, the choir director, provided impetus for soaring spirits with his constant exhortation that we "sing with the spirit and with understanding also." His inspiring messages before our concerts on cross-country tours frequently provided a spiritual setting which left hardly any choir member's eyes dry.

Prayer became increasingly important to me during the years. Throughout those seven years in preparation for the ministry I never found it difficult to experience spiritual enrichment. In addition to the daily devotional services and scripture reading,

I escaped the noise, smoke, and restlessness of the dormitory by gathering up my cards of Greek vocabulary, Shakespeare poetry, and chemical formulas and walking through the peaceful forests and hills surrounding the college. These "study" excursions often ended in earnest prayer to the Lord for guidance and strength.

Pastor Pieplow had instilled in me the desire for service. That desire led to my joining the Mission Society on campus. Some of us in the Mission Society had our own personal reasons for making the two-mile walk each Saturday from our campus to the state hospital. For me it was a type of therapy which I craved—an experience which made me thankful for my strong body, mind, and spirit. I discovered in these "children" a compensation for their mental retardation much like a blind or deaf person has. That compensation or reward was spiritual acceleration. What childlike faith these childlike adults possessed! I never pitied their condition; rather, I envied their exuberant faith and their enthusiasm for gospel religion.

Although I apparently had every reason to be satisfied with my decision to give my life to the ministry, I was almost constantly troubled with doubts. I had constantly experienced what I began to call an "Elijah syndrome." This syndrome is a feeling almost everyone experiences in life at one time or another, and to me it is epitomized by two passages from the "Elijah" oratorio by Felix Mendelssohn: "It is enough, O Lord, now take away my life," and "I go on my way in the strength of the Lord." Because of this attitude I experienced the depression which was followed by the accident I mentioned previously. The Lord made quite clear to me that escape was not the answer to my problems.

I was soon convinced by my professors and counselors that the accident had been a sure sign of God's wish for me to continue my studies. And continue I did. However, each following year I still sought further escape, though unsuccessfully. I spent parts of two summers in Europe. Spiritual peace eluded me. In senior college I almost forgot about God through my activities and involvement, without being aware of what I was doing. I was carrying a heavy academic load, singing in two choirs, directing a third, and acting as chairman of the Mission Committee on campus.

My search for truth, wisdom, and knowledge was insatiable. I read books whenever the titles intrigued me, and I found that these books set before me further steppingstones in many directions, heights and depths. In this light, it is amazing that I had not bothered to learn about Mormonism earlier, particularly after a chapel talk on November 8, 1963, given by a former Salt Lake City Protestant pastor. My journal reads, "Pastor Bruning had a very hilarious, yet soul-enlightening talk on Mormonism. I was very interested in it."

Closely aligned with this search for knowledge was the use of the talents with which I had been blessed and which I had developed as a result of my excellent Lutheran education and background. I could not see why I shouldn't utilize to the fullest in the ministry my music, art, foreign languages, and counseling ability. Indeed, many pastors forgot their Greek, Hebrew, and Latin when they had received their first call to a parish. I felt keenly that I would be condemned if I did not develop my talents.

Lack of confidence in myself and nagging doubts were, I believed, the worst stumbling blocks I encountered. Questions which plagued me constantly were: Where is God? What is the purpose of life? How does one follow in the footsteps of Christ? I felt that something was missing, but I knew not what it was. It took a long time for me to discover the important missing gospel principle, but even when I was confronted by its absence it did not occur to me. During the summer of 1966 I again had the opportunity to go to Europe. While staying at the youth hostel in Zurich, Switzerland, I found myself involved in religious discussions with young people of many nationalities and faiths— atheistic and agnostic, Christian, and Muslim. Even though I had been studying for the ministry I felt extremely uncomfortable and could not answer many of their theological and philosophical questions. Furthermore, I could not sincerely stand up for my beliefs. In short, I lacked a testimony. I also realized that others viewed the ministry of any church as an unnecessary, Middle Ages-vintage job with security, free time, and affluence abounding. I myself had to admit that there were too many ministers leading that type of life.

I was far from being perfect, but at least I had the desire to search for truth and improve myself. Once I had graduated I could not help but reflect upon seven years of preparation possibly wasted. It required prayer and a summer of awareness around less-educated men of many faiths to lead me to the conclusion that something was amiss. The churches with which I was familiar were not fulfilling the spiritual needs of their members; rather, their leaders preferred to quarrel among themselves concerning every absurd interpretation of every irrelevant doctrine, leaving in their wake contradictory concepts, heart-rending conventions, and confused members. I wondered what would happen if Christ should come to earth now. With me, he would wonder why theologians would call God a being without passions, yet turn around and call him compassionate. He would also see the churches too full of the manifestations of the weaker side of the human cultural evolution; that is, senseless rituals, superstitions, and plain magic (like buying one's salvation). After seeing the myths built up around him—the false creeds, the denominationalism and sacramentalism—he would surely remark, "If this is Christianity, I am not a Christian." He might have agreed with Malcolm X, who said, "I'm in a society that might preach brotherhood on Sunday, but they don't *practice* it on no day."

Whenever I donned the surplice and cassock to assist in the liturgy or preach a sermon, I felt a certain aesthetic power and a feeling that I was greatly respected by the congregation. At first I considered it an extreme sensation of spirituality, but now I know it was only a superficial feeling of majesty. Likewise, church architecture left me cold and stony, for it contributed to a great aesthetic atmosphere, giving one the same emotional feelings one receives when visiting a great European cathedral, but the atmosphere lacked a feeling of being close to God. I became very weary of these superficialities and yearned to find experiential faith somewhere.

Many times I had been discouraged in my efforts. I remember trying to help a girl who had considered suicide. My counselor advised me not to get involved. That lack of concern for the lives of others bothered me very much, but I persisted, finally

152   No More Strangers

succeeding in getting Toni on her knees in prayer. In my experience I have found that Christians believed in prayer, but not
in the power of prayer. The sophistries of men dictate wonderful
topics for theological discussions, but I was not interested in
wasting life discussing theology. I was more in favor of living
the gospel. It became increasingly difficult for me to tell where
truth lay, for current exegetical processes are rational and scientific rather than revelatory or inspirational. As a matter of
fact, many Christians cannot conceive of inspiration from the
Holy Spirit despite the fact of their belief in his existence.

Other questions which plagued me constantly had to do with
the lack of Pentecostalism in my church; the theology of grace
and faith alone; the graphic isolation of biblical events; the
negative rather than the positive view of man's existence; and
the salvation of non-Christians who had never had the opportunity of hearing the message of the gospel. The latter problem
intrigued me so much that I studied other non-Christian religions,
discovering that many of their beliefs paralleled my own. As
little as one month before my conversion to The Church of Jesus
Christ of Latter-day Saints I was planning a newsletter in cooperation with my friends at Concordia Senior College wherein we
were to express our concerns for the spiritual "Black Hole" the
church was in. An article was also in the process of being
written when I was baptized into the Church.

One summer evening in 1968, as I knelt in my local church
in Kendallville, Indiana, I poured out my heart to God, finally
realizing that there is power in prayer if one has the faith.
The many questions I had previously entertained began to be
answered, and the Lord provided guidance and assurance along
the way. After one of the most difficult decisions I have ever
made, I withdrew my name from the admissions office at the
theological seminary.

After volunteering for service in the army, I was called
to Indianapolis for physicals, tests, and other paper work. At the
end of the day the examining doctor informed me that I was not
fit for the army because of a congenital back defect. Discouraged, I walked back to the bus depot for the return trip to

Kendallville. On a hunch I took a detour to the Indianapolis Public Library and talked to the personnel director. He informed me that a position would open soon in the Arts Division, and he felt that I was qualified for it. I applied for the opening, and two months later I began what turned out to be part of my life's work. Now I was able to satisfy my thirst for knowledge in religion, art, music, languages, and literature as well as help other people find it.

After beginning my work at the library, I spent the following months "playing at church," searching for truth in various denominations throughout Indianapolis. Hindsight informs me that the churches I attended the most were those with the best music, organs, and choirs. How watered-down my faith had become! Friday night, December 13, 1968, found me "guarding the books" alone in the Arts Division. A graduate student in music walked in requesting some help in research for a paper. Although I had never seen Lyn Ruhland before, I immediately felt that I had known her all my life. As we became acquainted she informed me that she was LDS, and to my surprise that did not bother me. I thought she could be converted to the Lutheran Church.

Before meeting Lyn I had not had the desire to learn more about these Mormons whom I had been taught "were sent from Satan to lead astray the righteous." Lyn, who is now my wife, offered to "protect" me as I visited her church, a church which was like no other I had visited. The members of the ward were friendly and did not try to shove Mormonism down my throat. This alone was enough to convince me to listen to the missionaries. Through them I learned the truth about the personality of God and man's relationship to him, the saving principles and ordinances of the gospel, the priesthood of God, and continuing revelation. I found that this Church possessed the fulness of the gospel for which I had been seeking and also a prophet to guide its people. I also discovered that many basic LDS doctrines varied little from those of the Lutheran Church. A passage in the Book of Mormon clearly substantiates several New Testament teachings which provide the core of many Protestant faiths: ". . . For ye have not come thus far save it were by the words of Christ with unshaken faith in him, relying wholly upon the merits of him who is mighty to save." (2 Nephi 31:19.)

My landlady would not allow the missionaries into her home; consequently, I listened in Lyn's apartment to the spiritual message the elders had for me. During the course of the discussions Lyn read a forensics essay which I had written four years earlier concerning the will of God for his people. Her comment was, "You've been a Mormon all along and didn't know it!" The light of Christ must have been strong at times in those earlier days, for I remember giving little sermonettes in dormitory devotions which I subsequently realized were distinctly LDS in doctrine and spirit. I was not able to understand at the time why I received so much criticism, for I felt that I was preaching what I knew to be the truth; yet it was contrary to Lutheran theology.

Good works and miraculous deeds are not the only fruits by which I came to know the "Mormons," for the Holy Spirit bore witness to the truthfulness of the gospel. Thus I could not go against my conscience any more than Luther could go against his. I realized that no one can prove the truthfulness of religion by reason, intellect, or the scientific method, for true religion can only be revealed to man from God. Moroni, one of the prophets of ancient America, wrote: "By the power of the Holy Ghost ye may know the truth of all things." (Moroni 10:5.) I saw this as an excellent exhortation in these days when false teachings are rampant throughout the world.

I tried vainly to disprove the Book of Mormon, but each time I read parts of it I knew that it had to be the word of God. No reasonable explanation exists except that it was brought to Joseph Smith under the direction of the Lord to be translated for our benefit and as a witness that Christ is the Son of God and the Redeemer of the world. To the anti-Mormon claim that the Book of Mormon is a fraud, let me merely say that it is impossible for an objective scholar to hold this view. A *truly* objective scholar is by definition open-minded and would recognize the words in the Book of Mormon as constituting the word of God.

Being confronted with the LDS Church gave me the opportunity to learn of an organization I had always thought of as non-Christian and full of hoaxes. Though I felt this way about it at first, it soon became apparent that I had to join the Church, even though I knew this would bring sorrow to my dear parents, who held the same misconceptions about the Church which I had previously harbored. One important factor in forsaking family, friends, and former beliefs was the missionaries. I like to believe that mine were special. Elders Fuller and Moon had a testimony of Christ stronger than I had ever known in anyone, and it was certainly exercised during those moments when I wanted to side-track them.

But prayer was the foremost instrument in my spiritual conversion. I had always been taught to pray, but I had never been taught the power of prayer as Mormons know it. Prayer was particularly important when Satan began to try me three months after my baptism. I had gotten interested in an anti-Mormon writing, and it had given me some negative feelings about the Church. My home teachers were deeply concerned over my feelings but did not pressure me. Instead, they exhorted me to pray and fast. I did so, and in addition Lyn stayed up with me all night discussing points which had confused me in the book I was reading. The outcome was that I received an even stronger testimony of the gospel of Jesus Christ.

How wonderful it is to be a member of the Church revealed by the Lord himself as a restoration of the early Christian church! The Jews had been blinded by false teachers, rejecting both Moses and Christ. Many cults arose after the Savior's resurrection, distorting the simple gospel. Now I knew that there was no Savior but Jesus, and that he saves only in his own straight and narrow way and not according to man-made creeds and liturgies. It was refreshing to hear laymen preach and bear witness to the truthfulness of the gospel. As I listened, many times I could not help but be reminded of Paul's sermons during his missionary journeys in Derbe, Lystra, and Rome.

As I grew in my understanding of the gospel's principles I began to understand matters which previously had been beyond my grasp. I learned that to be resurrected and immortal is not all that is required for entrance into eternal life in the kingdom of

God. Eternal life in that kingdom is far beyond God's universal gift of immortality and is his greatest gift to all mankind. It can only be brought about through obedience to the doctrines and commandments taught by Jesus Christ. When I joined the Church I received a spiritual testimony long before I received any kind of intellectual testimony, but now I can say that I have both plus a testimony as solid as rock based on my experience in living the commandments.

Being baptized into The Church of Jesus Christ of Latter-day Saints did not make my life any easier. During the first three years as a member I felt deep remorse that I had hurt my parents, even though I knew within my own heart that what I had done was the right thing. The only things my loved ones and friends knew about the Church, unfortunately, had come from non-Mormon friends and anti-Mormon literature. Some of them apparently forgot that I was once studying for the ministry. I was therefore aware of my own former convictions and well acquainted with the *a-priori* assumptions and misconceptions taught concerning Mormonism. These false teachings are usually derived from ignorance of the truth and blind ecclesiocentrism, neither of which has any positive relationship with faith in the Lord Jesus Christ or with one's soul. Since my critical friends did not accept that book, I was not able to quote the Book of Mormon to them. But I used James 1:5 in trying to turn them from darkness to light. When threatened with excommunication from my former church, I gave my consent, informing them that their excommunication would not be any more effective for me than it was for Martin Luther, he too having become aware that the church no longer had authority to perform such acts. Furthermore, I was and am fully aware of the responsibilities and consequences should my decision prove to be wrong, but there is no doubt in my mind concerning the restoration of the gospel.

As free human beings we pride ourselves on the fact that everyone has a right to his own opinion, but my experiences have emphasized that where religion is concerned opinion is not enough to help us. We need the Holy Spirit. Otherwise, we begin to harbor threadbare beliefs and questions, enveloping our whole outlook in a sort of tortoise-like shell of protective belief. This shuts out the Spirit of truth and puts us in the position Paul described in his first letter to the Corinthians: "But the natural man receiveth not the things of the Spirit of God: for they are foolishness unto him: neither can he know them, because they are spiritually discerned." (1 Corinthians 2:14.)

My family meant well. They expressed deep concern for me, and I am thankful for their love — love great enough to worry that much about me. To them, I had embraced the biggest fraud ever known. My mother once told me that my grandmother would live until she saw me a minister. That was a force in her desire to live. If her interpretation of being a minister is that I serve God and my fellowman, I can sincerely answer that I have met her goal for me. In the midst of my investigating the Church my parents grieved so much that it brought them to their knees in prayer many times in my behalf. My mother later wrote and told me of the testimony she received that "Gary is in good hands." What a witness to receive! It could easily be her own testimony.

The experiences surrounding my conversion underlined the fact that the religious world in general worships the learning of man and trusts in the arm of flesh. They hold man's reasoning in greater esteem than God's revelations; and for the most part they do not even believe in the power of God to reveal his will to man. A dichotomy exists which symbolizes the basic difference between other Christian faiths and Mormonism—creative theology versus revealed theology. Creative theology can be a dogmatic and philosophical system of theology but not a revealed one. The application of the principles taught by Jesus Christ points in one direction, not in several.

> And if your eye be single to my glory, your whole bodies shall be filled with light, and there shall be no darkness in you; and that body which is filled with light comprehendeth all things. (D&C 88:67.)

Enthusiastically following God's laws was a change for me. Earlier in my life "law" meant unrelenting, cruel authority. It had come to mean the opposite of fun. But the Hebrew word for *law* in the Old Testament, *Torah*, is derived from a Hebrew word which is akin to the word for light. Putting all the concepts together, I found that God's law is a course of instruction which causes man to see the light of God's truth and thereby receive blessings. The law is designed for the purpose of bringing man from the carnal, human level of thinking and existing to the higher level. Laws are no legalistic nooses around our necks, as many believe about our Church disciplines, but a means whereby we can become really free. Martin Luther's treatise on the freedom of the Christian man is only a beginning.

The restoration of the gospel—how beautifully this concept was described by a Lutheran theologian and minister from a Nazi prison in 1944, who never knew the restored gospel during his mortal life!

> The doctrine of the restoration of all things is a magnificent conception, full of comfort; nothing is lost, everything is taken up in Christ, although it is transformed, made transparent, clear and free from all selfish desire. Christ brings this to us again, as intended by God originally, without the distortion by our sins. (Dietrich Bonhoeffer, *Letters From Prison*)

I bear my testimony that God lives today; that I have felt his influence for good in my life as well as his presence many times. I know that I found greater understanding of myself and of life in general as I discarded fixed ideas that were once imposed upon me. I outgrew fears and depressions as an understanding of the gospel developed within me. Previously life was largely a succession of uncertainties—of possible failure in education, of being ill, of being lonely. Yet when I began to understand the meaning of life and made an avid and determined study and practice of the gospel, uncertainties were for the most part eliminated.

I am grateful to know that our Father in heaven has sent us prophets and apostles to lead us in the last days. I can also say with all soberness that the present President of the Church is as much a prophet of God as were Moses and Elijah. I know that Jesus Christ is the Redeemer of the world. God grant that we may all continually increase in faith and in our ability to keep the commandments, all of which he has given us for our own good.

Coby Van Mastrigt

THE COURAGE TO PURSUE

*No thinking person goes through life on continually calm
waters. There are varying pressures, unresolved problems, baffling
questions. And everyone has basic needs and desires which must
be satisfied before he can be happy.*

*One of the greatest voids in anyone's life is revealed through
the divine discontent, the sacred longing, the unsatisfied hunger
of the soul. This can be satisfied only through discovering the
gospel.*

*But even then, when faith is fragile the answers can bring
concern, even fears sparked by a new round of questions.*

*Do I have the courage to pursue new knowledge and then
abide by it the rest of my days?*

*Why should I persist in the weary struggle for truth when
conformity with the standards around me would seem so much
easier?*

*In a world where Satan has had so much power for centuries
and there are so many ideologies, how do I know for sure that
I have found the truth, this time?*

*These were some of the concerns which Wim and Coby Van
Mastrigt experienced, having already been exposed to several
disappointing ideologies. This account shows how conversion
answered such questions.*

———————

In May 1940, eight months after the outbreak of World
War II, our resident city of Rotterdam, Netherlands, was all but
leveled by a German air raid. At this time I was seventeen years

old and my future husband Wim (then unknown to me) was twenty years old and in pilot training in the Royal Dutch Air Force.

After our country had been occupied by enemy forces, several underground movements were organized and both Wim and I became heavily involved in this cause. We met for the first time during an underground meeting in March of 1941. Wim was very upset to find a girl in that type of activity and he urged me to go home and leave those matters to the men. This advice I elected to ignore. From that time on we were almost inseparable.

The time came when the U.S.A. entered the war and allied herself with Russia. This alliance baffled my husband. Why would a country like the U.S.A. join a master criminal to defeat a small criminal like Hitler? We in Holland already knew of Russian concentration camps and purges. We knew that what the Germans had done in their country in this respect was only a small-scale imitation of what the Russians had been doing for decades.

Our observation that national governments conspire with each other without the knowledge of the people led us to investigate history and governments. Research led us into the study of activities of secret societies and subversive organizations. We could not then know that the Book of Mormon would explain that very subject to us twenty-five years later.

The war and the subsequent German occupation of Holland was a most difficult experience for us both. During the occupation, many of the Dutch people had good reasons to hide from the Germans. For one thing, the Jews among us knew they would lose their lives if they were found, just because they were Jews. For political reasons, most of the other citizens had to be very cautious in order to avoid arrest.

Food was rationed at the time, and in order to obtain food for refugees it became necessary for many people to forge ration cards. Conditions forced me to secure food by riding my bike for many miles, bargaining directly with farmers. They sold me food either for money or for articles such as sheets, towels, salt, or gold jewelry. More often than not these articles of value were more acceptable to farmers than money because money didn't have any value during those days.

For a time I was hospitalized with wounds I received when a British plane strafed a truck which had given a lift to me and my bikeload of provisions.

Wim was convicted and sentenced to twenty-nine months of hard labor on the charge of possessing a radio and listening to the British radio broadcasts. (Both were illegal acts at the time.) When his attorney said that nothing more could be done for him, it was suggested that he try an escape by tricking the Germans into releasing him as skilled labor. The Germans at that time (early 1944) had a desperate need in their war industry for technically skilled labor. Once Wim was released for work he would go into hiding and, we hoped, not be found again. The plan worked. He was given permission to go home for one week to get clothes and other necessities.

Wim's physical condition was extremely poor and even a German doctor diagnosed some fourteen or so maladies. In these circumstances some time was allowed for recuperation. We deemed it unwise to go into hiding as long as he could stay home "legally." Finally, around the end of August or the beginning of September 1944, he was told to report for work on the following Saturday. We immediately started preparations for him to travel to the hiding place for which I had arranged earlier. Forged ration cards and a passport were provided. Before the appointed Saturday arrived, however, "Mad Tuesday" occurred. Rumors of pending Allied invasion sent Germans and quislings alike into a panic. The resulting exodus of these enemies enabled the Dutch underground organization to destroy German offices and burn most of the records. We never heard of the matter again, even when most of the Germans who had left returned to Holland.

When the war ended, Wim went back to school to finish his studies as an engineer and we were married. Holland had emerged from the war as a socialist state and in our view this was not the right environment in which to raise a family. We felt that the government had too much power over the individual citizen, affecting his life every day to the point that it became oppressive.

We considered ourselves capable of making our own decisions and felt we did not need anyone, least of all a government, to do that for us. Basically, we wanted to be free and independent. My husband was desperately anxious to emigrate to the U.S.A. where, we thought, there was true freedom and where the people appreciated their freedom and would never be so careless as to let it be threatened. Perhaps we were naive at the time.

On the day our third child was born in 1950, we received an invitation from an American company for which Wim had worked briefly in Holland, asking him to come to Cleveland, Ohio, and work there. He had applied for emigration to the U.S.A. in August 1945, as soon as the American Consulate was reopened in Rotterdam, and by this time the visa application was ready and a quota number issued. Wim left Holland in February 1951 and I followed him with three small children in June of that year. We settled our family in Ohio.

At the time we witnessed our first election (we were not yet U.S. citizens), we noticed to our amazement that most of our neighbors did not even take the trouble to vote. This was our first disappointment in America.

In the meantime, our eldest boy had started school. With a conviction copied from our own parents, Wim and I started with the premise that a teacher knows best what is good for children and that a wise parent should not interfere with a teacher's judgment or the school's policy. It was not long however before our son started to come home with assignments which both my husband and I considered dangerous to his morale. These assignments did not involve things which were of themselves big and important, in fact the matters concerned would have escaped the attention of almost any parent unless he had been conditioned to recognize them. We felt that they were an attempt to invade privacy of opinion through homework assignments. Past experience taught us that such things would slowly erode the sanctity of the family and the home, thereby undermining our influence upon our children and eventually destroying the privacy we valued so much.

I am sure that the teachers were for the most part totally

unaware of these implications and, in the Lutheran school at least, were dedicated to the welfare of our children. Even so, when we attempted to help them understand what we thought about the educational methods being used and what results they invited, we met with strong resistance. The teachers' attitude seemed to be that they were the experts and we were the naive parents who did not know anything. Despite this, we remained convinced that the methods we complained of were causing the erosion of moral character, of love and respect for God, country, and life itself.

As time went on and our children advanced in school, the seriousness of these offenses against our judgment increased steadily. In the meantime we had moved to California. With the battle for our children's minds in full swing, life was far from easy; especially for our children, who by now were beginning to think for themselves. Their parents stood alone against the schools and the community and were considered nuisances.

Now that that is all behind us, we know that the battle was worth while, for as a result our children learned to think clearly and logically. They have grown up with sound values and a love of their country. Nevertheless it is a sad experience for us as a family when we consider the many boys and girls who have neither been taught to select right over wrong nor have the strength to stick to their convictions once they have made the selection. Many of the youngsters who grew up in our neighborhood have fallen into illegal drug use, and some have even lost their lives in the process.

It did not take us very long to become disenchanted with the Lutheran Church, where the social gospel seemed to be taking the upper hand. We began to investigate every church and religion we heard of. (For some reason The Church of Jesus Christ of Latter-day Saints did not come to our attention.) Some of these religions appeared to have a lot to offer, but as we got deeper into each it was never long before we became dissatisfied. It just seemed that whichever church we looked at, we always ended up finding the undesirable things, and there was never enough good to offset the undesirable. We did not know it then, but all along we were experiencing the whisperings of the Spirit, and for some reason we usually heeded it no matter what the consequences. Perhaps too our early experiences among a conquered people during the war had made us particularly wary.

The years sped by while all around us we saw the same signs of decay in the schools and communities of our adopted country. In fact it seemed as if the whole world was in decline and headed for certain disaster. At that time we felt that the solution surely could be found in politics, but that turned out to be a fallacy; and if anything good came out of the gloomy experiences of this period it was the lessons we learned when we dabbled in politics. Politics without high moral values and without spiritual guidance clearly leads always to a worsening rather than an improvement in local as well as national affairs.

Our experiences were such that I, at least, became bitter toward other people and finally reached the point where, for the first time in my life, I seriously began to doubt the wisdom of my convictions. I even began to rationalize that perhaps I should start living as everybody else did and go along with the crowd. Through all the years of struggle, my peace of mind had never once really left me until this time. Now I had hit rock bottom. It was at this point that some very interesting and unusual things began to happen to me.

One afternoon I was reading a book about the dangers facing America, one of countless books I had read on this subject. While I was reading I had a strange but real experience. It was as if a film began to unroll before me and suddenly I knew that all of those things which Wim and I had been opposing for so long were not, as we had always believed, the work of evil men alone, but the work of Satan. At the same time it was revealed to me that, since this was so, it followed that the opposition to Satan's plan must exist. Therefore, the Lord's plan must be just as real. I knew now that somewhere upon this earth the true Church of the Lord existed.

The questions were: Where do we find this Church? What is it called? Whom do we contact? I did not have the faintest idea where to look for it. Probably for the first time in my life,

I began to pray seriously for an answer to a specific question. It took several weeks before the answer began to come, and even then it came very slowly.

During a meeting we held at our house, someone brought a friend whom I had not previously met. At the end of the meeting I offered coffee and cake. When this lady refused coffee I asked her why. She said she was a Mormon. The many questions that followed prompted this lady to send the missionaries to our home.

During the period of my confusion and doubt, my husband also had been experiencing some of the same or similar problems. Although he never doubted the wisdom of his convictions, he had been disappointed and disillusioned often enough not to want to meet with the missionaries at that time. But he kept the door open by telling me to let him know if I found anything really important.

Right from the start the missionaries knew that I was what they called a "golden contact." Everything they taught me I knew was true. It went right along with my own thinking in many respects. Therefore, being young and enthusiastic, they naturally tried to set a date for my baptism. What they did not know was that my scars were deep. The idea of having to make a decision before I knew all the facts frightened me, and I told them that I did not want to meet them again. How disappointed they must have been! I no longer even remember their names. I wish they could know how well they did their work.

Almost immediately after this I started reading and studying the doctrines of the LDS Church. It was not long before my husband also dropped everything to pursue the same study. Together we discussed the many exciting things we found. Even so, our attitude was that we were determined to find any crack there might be in the foundation. If this was the true gospel we had found, it would contain no faults or errors. But we had to scrutinize it carefully and make sure that in accepting it we would not be repeating mistakes of the past by joining an organization which was instituted by man and would prove to be a disappointment.

It took us two years of study, primarily concentrated on the standard works of the Church. The Book of Mormon in particular began slowly to penetrate and enlarge our understanding. Stake missionaries met with us a few times and they were instrumental in getting us to Sunday School classes.

A part of the Book of Mormon which particularly impressed us was 3 Nephi 7, in which the chief judge is murdered and the government overthrown. With President Kennedy's assassination still fresh in mind, and with attacks constantly being made on the Constitution, the modern U.S. scene had striking parallels with that Nephite situation. We were impressed too by 3 Nephi 8-10, which indicates that, when Christ was crucified and went to the spirit world, all light ceased to exist upon the earth, and that it only returned when Christ was resurrected. The three days of absolute darkness hold a very important lesson for us today in that when Christ is not here (speaking not only figuratively but also literally) light ceases to exist.

Most impressive to my husband was the record of the Jaredites, especially what is written in Ether 8:18-25 about secret combinations. Verse 22 says that "whatsoever nation shall uphold such secret combinations, to get power and gain, until they shall spread over the nation, behold, they shall be destroyed."

We read the warning to serve God contained in Ether 2:9-10, verse 10 of which says: "For behold, this is a land which is choice above all other lands, wherefore he that doth possess it shall serve God, or they shall be swept off." Because the U.S.A. is part of that choice land, we felt, in it "it is not right that any man should be in bondage one to another." (D&C 101:79.) Verse 80 told us of the divine inspiration behind the Constitution: "And for this purpose have I established the Constitution of this land, by the hands of wise men whom I raised up unto this very purpose, and redeemed the land by the shedding of blood."

Our studies made clear to us that the events implied by that verse had to take place before the gospel could be reestablished. It appears that the Lord tried several times to make the American continent his showcase where his children would live by the gospel laws and ordinances. After Adam and Eve and the flood came the time of the Jaredites, but they fell away from the commandments of God and finally exterminated themselves. At about the time the Jaredite civilization ended, the Lord caused Lehi and Ishmael with their families to leave Palestine for America. The Book of Mormon tells the story of the Nephite civilization up to the time that the Nephites were annihilated by the Lamanites at the battle around the Hill Cumorah in about A.D. 385.

Before the Lord tried the next time, he created an atmosphere where his gospel at least would have a chance to survive. He knew the civilizations can expand and prosper only as far as their respective forms of government allow. Therefore, he inspired the creation of a republic in 1776 which had to prove itself by revolution and war before the restoration of the gospel could take place. It was not until 1820 that Joseph Smith had his first vision. Ten years later the Church was restored.

It is this sequence of events that to us was all-important in understanding the intents of the Lord.

All this preparation and understanding and clarification, and more that I have not detailed, was necessary before we could accept the gospel with the full knowledge that it is what we had been searching for during all those years and that nothing in the future could change our minds, regardless of circumstances or consequences.

I found no peace of mind until I found The Church of Jesus Christ of Latter-day Saints. When I was satisfied it was the one true Church, I announced to my husband that, no matter what he did, I just had to be baptized. He told me he was not yet ready to be baptized, although he admitted that it was only a matter of time. He admonished me that, if I wanted to go ahead, I had to go all the way in all the things the Church expected of me. The last thing he said in this conversation was: "And don't ever come telling me you can't afford to pay the tithe." So I went ahead and asked the lady missionaries to make arrangements for my baptism.

I was to be interviewed for baptism the day before being baptized. On Friday morning, my husband gave me a shock by telling me he did not want the missionaries to come for the interview during that day. What he meant, fortunately, was that they had better come in the evening so that he also could be interviewed. We never for one moment have regretted our decision.

One year after our baptism, my husband and I were sealed in the Oakland Temple for time and eternity.

During our search our children, all of them in their teens, watched their parents with many misgivings as we tried once more to find "it." No doubt, after all they had seen, they had little faith that we would be successful. On the other hand, being conscious that we had subjected them to many different doctrines already, my husband and I were very anxious not to appear to force them into joining the Church. We asked our friends, old and new, to leave our children alone and do nothing that might turn them against the Church. Maybe we were too careful, for although every so often one or the other would have a question, which we would then discuss in detail, nothing happened to even give us hope that the children would be converted.

Then suddenly my husband's company transferred him to Ankara, Turkey, for an engineering assignment. There we found a small branch of about seventy-five members, primarily U.S. military people. We were active from the time of our arrival. It was here that we met another Dutchman who believed strongly that a family should be united in the Church. Thanks to his efforts, our children received a crash course of instruction. He had only two weeks left before he was transferred to Indonesia. Every evening after dinner, there he was, giving all of his precious time to our children. Without my husband or me interfering in any manner, the three children who were with us in Turkey decided in about a week's time that they wanted to be baptized. So on a cold Saturday morning in January we managed to get an air force bus with a Turkish driver to carry the entire branch over icy roads to Kizilkahamam hot springs for our children's baptisms.

A baptism in Turkey is a major physical undertaking. There are no indoor baptismal fonts or even swimming pools. (For one baptism, on another occasion, we had to go three hundred miles to the Mediterranean Sea on the south coast of Turkey.) The only reason we were able to get facilities in Kizilkahamam, which is about sixty miles from Ankara on the way to Istanbul, was that the only Turkish member in our branch made arrangements with the mayor of Kizilkahamam for a Turkish bath to be used by a group of Americans. Since the Turks do not swim and certainly do not bathe in mixed groups, bystanders looked on in amazement as the entire busload of men, women, and children went into the bathhouse. All non-Moslem religious ceremonies are forbidden by law in Turkey, and this includes baptism. So although we went in under the guise of swimming, we did not swim. The bath house was unheated, though the temperature was a cold 20 degrees. We had our service, including the singing of a hymn, and then proceeded with the baptism proper. The water from a volcanic hot spring was scalding hot. Steam made everything so foggy that it was difficult to see whether the immersions were total. However, since the participants' skins were completely red from head to toe, we were sure that the ordinance had been performed properly.

When our oldest daughter returned to the U.S.A. that summer to attend Ricks College in Rexburg, Idaho, we drove our car to Amsterdam with the entire family. We then went to Switzerland, where we visited Zollikofen and had our children sealed to us in the Swiss Temple. (From Turkey, the other two children eventually went to Ricks College after they had finished their U.S. Air Force high school in Ankara.)

After our daughter left for America, I stayed in the Netherlands for almost two months, where I spent most of my time researching our ancestry in local libraries. I was able to find and identify several hundred persons in our genealogical lines. To us it is wonderful to be a small part of the atmosphere the Lord has created not only in restoring the gospel but also in providing temples where work can be done for everyone who did not have the privilege to partake of the saving ordinances in ages past. We feel very privileged and thankful that we can participate in these ordinances and assist in building Zion. Understanding the eternal nature of life, the knowledge that families will be united forever in the patriarchal order through the genealogical effort we expend in behalf of our ancestors—this is a tremendous blessing.

Many blessings have come to us since joining the Church, not the least being our children's enrollment in the excellent schools provided by the Church. We keep a very close contact with all of our children, and although we are frequently far away in distance, we feel joy and happiness in the knowledge that we will be able to live as a family for all eternity. Somehow the distance does not seem too important to us.

Since becoming members of the Church we have met some of the finest people ever. No matter where we have traveled we have met active members of the Church with whom we seem to have a certain tie. It is as if we had met them before, as if we had known each other. There never is a feeling of forced politeness but always one of closeness that is difficult to explain. It is as though we are of the same family.

Our conversion changed many things for us, but one thing which has not changed is our sincere concern for the future of the U.S.A. Everything we stand for and all that we value in terms of freedom is under attack and seems to be crumbling. Some of our member friends say that, after all, this is happening as a fulfillment of prophecy and therefore is inevitable. But we still have our free agency and perhaps we can be instrumental in helping to prevent the destruction of all that we love and cherish. My husband and I will seek by all legal and constitutional means to keep this land, the "land of the free and the home of the brave." That we may always obey the God of this land, who is Jesus Christ, we pray in the name of Jesus Christ, our Redeemer. Amen.

JANET THERESE MOLLOY

LIFE TRANSFORMED FOR NEW ZEALAND NUN

From the journal of Janet Molloy of New Zealand comes the moving story of her years as a nun and her conversion to The Church of Jesus Christ of Latter-day Saints.

Since several members of Janet's family whom she loves and respects are devoting exceptional service to the Catholic Church, severing herself from such a heritage was a difficult decision.

Drawing from the record she has kept of her life, she moves rapidly from the time she was a normal giggly girl into the deep spiritual experiences of a sensitive young woman making monumental but very lonely decisions. Her story exemplifies the joy we can receive when we have lived true to convictions received through the Holy Spirit, no matter what the cost or how difficult the decision may have been at the time.

———————

I was born of wonderful parents in October 1945, in Auckland, New Zealand, and was baptized a Catholic when only a few weeks old. My primary schooling was at the local parish school, where I enjoyed the excellent teaching and strict discipline of the sisters of St. Joseph.

St. Mary's in Auckland was the scene of my secondary school days, under the strict supervision of the sisters of Our Lady of Mercy. It is a beautiful old school with great traditions where my mother had received her training also. In 1960 I graduated to Form IV, and this was the beginning of my most enjoyable school year. My teacher was young and inexperienced, so with the help of my friends I endeavored to give this good nun plenty of excitement. For example, we lined the ceiling of our classroom with squashy grapes which plopped down at intermittent intervals. We were the funniest, smartest girls—or so we thought. Often our conversation showed a lack of respect for Sister. One day I went a little too far and put a tiny dead mouse on her chair. The next day I found myself in the principal's office being threatened with expulsion from the school. I came away a rather frightened, remorseful girl.

The next year was a more serious one for me. I had a new teacher whom I loved and I did everything I could to cooperate with her. As the end of the school year was approaching, however, I felt concerned because I did not know what I was going to do with my life. Sitting at an office typewriter did not appeal to me and the nursing profession too had lost its attraction for me.

One day, a very close friend of mine (a nun) asked me if I had ever considered giving my life to God in a special way, as she had done. My reply was a definite negative. Strangely enough, though, I went home that night and knelt by my bed and really prayed from my heart for the first time. Our family had always made a practice of family prayer at night, but this consisted of reciting several decades of the rosary. As I knelt there in the dark, fingering my rosary beads, I prayed to God for guidance and courage. Suddenly I felt a deep sense of peace and a closeness to God.

As the days passed by I grew more serious and reflective. Finally, I decided to make an appointment to see the mother superior of the order of nuns who had taught me. I felt that this was what the Lord wanted of me.

I was approaching my sixteenth birthday and I knew that this was the minimum age requirement to enter the convent. Reverend Mother was a petite woman—quite striking to look at. Her beautiful Irish complexion camouflaged her middle age. At the end of a thorough interview, this sweet woman looked at me kindly and told me that I could enter the Convent of Our Lady of Mercy as soon as I could arrange it. The tears which had held back until this time suddenly streamed shamelessly down my face, and as Reverend Mother kissed me goodbye, telling me to come on the following February 2, I felt a great surge of joy and peace inside me. I felt that this was what the Lord wanted me to do. My parents were extremely surprised at my news, but they felt very proud of me and in no way tried to prevent me or dissuade me.

On Friday, February 2, 1962, at 3:00 P.M my family drove me over to St. Mary's Navitiate, the training house for the new arrivals. Seven other girls older than myself were arriving that same day. After being welcomed by Reverend Mother and our future novice mistress, we were ushered into a side room where we donned the severe black habit and sheer black veil. This was to be our mode of dress for ten months while we studied the teachings of the Catholic Church and learned about convent life and the holy rule of the Sisters of Mercy. We were called "postulants" during this period. Our duties were as follows: We rose at 5:45 A.M. to thirty-three tolls of a bell, and twenty minutes later we were required to be in the chapel to recite the psalms of the office of the blessed Virgin Mary. From 6:30 until 7:00 A.M. we sat quietly in our *priedieux* (kneeling desks) and meditated on points of doctrine. This was followed by holy Mass. After Mass we took turns at preparing the porridge, toast, and tea for thirty nuns at breakfast. When the bell sounded, each nun would arise, genuflect before the altar, and with the others walk slowly in single file, hands clasped and eyes downcast, into the refectory for our first meal of the day. The rest of our day was spent in studying, lectures, and prayer, until 9:00 P.M. when the grand silence began.

My first year in the Order of Our Lady of Mercy was a really hard one. Under the strict discipline of my novice mistress I became less boisterous and more serious. My most vivid memory of convent life is of constant humiliation. Having to listen while my faults were explained was difficult for me, but I am thankful for those years which taught me to know myself as I am and not just as I would like to be.

On October 20, eleven of us (all postulants) were received as "brides of Christ" into the order as novices for a further two-year training period before taking vows. Dressed in bridal dresses and veils, we walked up the aisle of St. Patrick's Cathedral as the choir sang "Veni Sponsor Christi" ("Come, Spouse of Christ").

For the following two years we were engaged in domestic work in the laundry and kitchen. Twice a day our work was interrupted for lectures on doctrine. During this period of intense spiritual training we were not permitted to leave the convent premises except on urgent business, nor could we read or study anything of a secular nature. These were indeed serious and reflective years for me.

When the two years had passed we were again permitted to solicit approval of the community of nuns to take vows and be full professed members of the order. During the profession ceremony our white veil was replaced by a black one and we each received a brass crucifix to wear in the belt. The most significant part of the ceremony was our individual reading of our vows. Each of us in turn read aloud her pledge to live a life of "poverty" (by which we renounced our right of ownership), "chastity" (by which we relinquished the right to marry) and "obedience" (by which we were no longer subject to our own will, but to that of a superior). My profession motto was imprinted on my vows— "Elegi Abjecta" ("I choose to be an abject"). I desired to continually remind myself that without the Lord's help I was nothing.

A few weeks later we were assigned to Monte Cecilia Convent, which was surrounded by Catholic churches, convents, and monasteries and (ironically) looked down onto the Auckland Latter-day Saint Stake Center. For two years we traveled by day to Loreto Hall Teachers College; then in the evening, back at the convent, we received additional spiritual training. In December 1966 I graduated with my teaching certificate plus a diploma of moral and dogmatic theology.

In January 1967 I received my first teaching assignment— at a parish school in an Auckland suburb. My forty little children were a source of great joy and satisfaction to me. Our old classroom glowed with their handcrafts; our free periods were spent in sitting in the field singing to my guitar.

It was at this time, after several years of experiencing slight doubts that I began to have serious doubts as to whether the life of a nun was my true vocation. (Despite this, I in no way challenged the authenticity of the Catholic Church.) I felt that I could not exist without having children of my own. And how could I go through life—lonely in spite of companions—only able to see my family one hour each month, although they lived close by? I found too that I was becoming far too harsh on myself as far as the reach for perfection was concerned. I demanded an unrealistic amount of dedication from myself, and when inevitably I fell short at times it was difficult for me to forgive myself. There were other doubts also, but I tried to ignore them because I suspected they were motivated by weakness. I desperately wanted to be a strong, disciplined, and courageous person who would not give in to selfish and worldly desires. I seemed to hear a voice saying: "Sister, this life is not meant to be easy. You have sacrificed things of the world. Don't give in to disheartenment and weakness. Be strong and put up with opposition." But as the days and weeks went by, my doubts became stronger; and after much prayer I knew that I must have the courage to leave that way of life. After some personal opposition, I returned to secular life in June 1967.

The adjustments which followed were often almost more than I could bear. I had become a real introvert and very sensitive. I missed the religious routine of the convent, and often at night I would cry for hours because I felt I had made a wrong decision in leaving it. In retrospect, I recognize these feelings as instigated by the adversary.

Eventually I found a job as a receptionist typist and very slowly began to gain confidence. Dating was a frightening experience. I was very naive by worldly standards and just longed to meet someone who was spiritually minded. Then one evening at a dance I met a young man who seemed very different from the others. We communicated well and it thrilled me to find someone who did not smoke, drink, or swear, and who had high standards. It was several weeks before I discovered in horror that this man was a member of the "Mormon" Church.

We both realized the unhappy consequences of a marriage between two people of such opposing faiths. Each time we were together we would discuss religion, and it was obvious that neither of us was about to change his beliefs. It seemed inevitable that we would have to end our friendship, as we were becoming serious about each other. I went to services of his church, and although I was impressed by the spirit of the people, the doctrines seemed to me ridiculous. So after a rich and exciting year together we finally had to part.

It was a very sad time for me. Occasionally I would go to the LDS Church just to see this young man again. I had made friends with a member of the stake presidency and his lovely wife, and I spent many enjoyable hours in their home. At this time there were two fine missionaries staying at the president's home and they engaged me in deep discussions about religion—but I was very defensive of my Catholic beliefs. These elders impressed me with their enthusiasm and gentle spirit, but I always assured them most definitely that I could never embrace their faith.

One day the missionaries invited me to attend their quarterly stake conference and, after much persuasion, I consented. Unknown to them, my only motive was that I wanted to see my former sweetheart again. As I listened to the speakers that day and felt that undeniably strong spirit of the LDS gathering, I felt some of the Catholic draining out of me, leaving me extremely confused. As I was leaving the chapel, one of my missionary friends came up to me and said: "Jan, I will be leaving New Zealand in just ten days' time, as my two years are up. I would love to have the privilege of baptizing you before I return." I was extremely shocked at such a request; but I was touched by the sincerity and gentle spirit which emanated from him, so I just thanked him for his concern and told him I could never give up my strong beliefs.

At home that night, however, I prayed desperately to the Lord asking him to take away the very strong doubts that were welling up in my mind about the Catholic faith. I was afraid that my love for my young friend was influencing my desire to share his beliefs, and this worried me. Seeking help from the scriptures, I picked up my New Testament and read isolated passages from different parts. To my amazement, everything I read seemed to reinforce the teachings of the LDS Church.

I prayed so very hard that night and all the next day! My doubts about the Catholic faith were very strong by now. In fact, I believed the LDS Church was true. But I knew that I would not only have to *believe*—I must really *know* in my heart that it was true before I would ever have the strength to give up all that I had dedicated my life to and expose myself to the shocked reactions of family and friends, who certainly would think I was trying to change my beliefs to suit my romantic notions.

On the following day, while I was even more convinced, I felt I still could not make the tremendous decision involved in joining the Church. But I was about to receive help. While working at my desk, I received a phone call from a friend who told me that my former sweetheart had just become engaged to another girl. This was a startling surprise to me, but it was not as surprising as my reaction. Suddenly things seemed to fall into place. Instead of feeling hurt and disappointment, I experienced an overwhelming feeling of joy and peace. I wanted to run out into the main office and shout for joy. It was as though part of the veil had been removed for a tiny second and I was able to see into the future. It became obvious to me that I had not met the right man for me yet, as the Lord had great things ahead for me to do. Now I knew what it meant to have a testimony of the truth, for I knew with all my heart—without any doubt at all—that The Church of Jesus Christ of Latter-day Saints is the one true Church. It had been unmistakably revealed to me by the Holy Ghost. My new conviction and courage was and always will be a miracle to me—I cannot explain it.

The following weeks were full of change. Just three days after that miraculous day in my life I was immersed in the waters of baptism. Immediately afterwards I was confirmed a member of The Church of Jesus Christ of Latter-day Saints and received the gift of the Holy Ghost. My family were deeply shocked and distressed, and it almost broke my heart to see their deep hurt and their fear for my soul. They are so wonderful and so strong in their own belief in Catholicism that it was inconceivable to them that any member of our large family could renounce the faith—especially one who had been a nun. Only a miracle could have brought me through the heart-rending weeks and months which ensued, but my testimony was so very strong that I could not deny it or compromise in any way.

It especially distressed my family that I would join the Church before I had even received any formal teaching about it. Although a spiritual testimony is powerful to the recipient, it is difficult for him to describe it. I admitted to my family that I had not learned everything about the Church, but I told them I could not deny its truth. Certainly if I had not known it was true I would not have put myself or them through the agony of that period.

Six months after my baptism I left New Zealand to attend Brigham Young University, and the following two years preceding my graduation in May 1972 were the most wonderful and action-packed years of my life. That beautiful university is indeed the Lord's and I felt the spirit there. On my first morning on campus I was overcome with the wonderful spirit which pervaded. Refined and well-groomed students rushed to and fro making cheerful comments to each other. Such a beautiful spirit! The chimes played "There is an Hour of Peace and Rest." The gospel meant so much to me and I thirsted for knowledge about it. I thrilled to study it in all its aspects under trained spiritual priesthood holders. My major field of study was in the social and family sciences, and I was very motivated to learn as much as I could. The more I studied, the greater my testimony of the gospel became. Everything I learned seemed to fit into the one eternal whole and I experienced a great sense of peace.

Sometimes Latter-day Saints ask me how I feel about the years I spent as a nun. I feel that I had been guided to train as a nun, even in a temporary situation. In those six years my spiritual nature was formed and a concern for deeper things was initiated. That is where I learned to pray, meditate, read, and study the scriptures. But for this training, I fear I would have been a very worldly person and I seriously doubt if I ever would have been attracted by the truth. In fact, I can't imagine what I would have been like if I had not had those years.

In January 1971 I was privileged to receive my endowments in the Salt Lake Temple. This was a very choice experience for me. When I left that beautiful house of the Lord that day, I knew as I had never known before that there is only one Church on this earth today in which the truth can be found, and I knew I had found that Church. Perhaps because of my unusual background, I experienced no doubts or difficulties—everything fitted into its place. The doctrine of the preexistence (so new to me) was the most beautiful doctrine I had ever heard of; and it thrilled me then and still does to know that I lived with my Heavenly Father before coming to this earth. My life now had so much more significance and meaning, and the joy I felt was inexpressible.

I am so thrilled by the encouragement one receives in the Church—such a positive attitude prevails, with no practice of humiliation. It is a way of life akin to our real natures—cheerful and loving. The gospel is consistent with fun, happiness, and real joy.

Before returning to my homeland in June of 1972, I had the privilege of visiting Nauvoo, Carthage and Liberty Jails, Adam-ondi-Ahman, and many other places of historical significance to Latter-day Saints. I will never forget the feeling I experienced as I sat in the room at Carthage Jail where Joseph Smith, our beloved Prophet, was martyred. Each of the visitors in that room with me that day experienced that same feeling, and we left in tears. How lucky we were to know the truth!

Since returning to New Zealand, I have been privileged to work for the Lord at the Church Distribution Center for the South Pacific at Auckland, New Zealand, with fifty other choice Latter-day Saints. As I witness the programs and progress of the Church and the great spirit of this latter-day work, again my testimony is greatly strengthened. I know that the Lord's work will never fail. It thrills me to see the progress of the Church in my homeland.

As I review these past four years, I am overwhelmed by the many wonderful blessings I have received. I know with all my heart that this Church is true because it has been revealed to me by the Holy Ghost. I also know this with my mind, because I have studied the gospel and have satisfied myself that it is without error. I know that God lives and I love him with all my heart and feel very close to him. He is indeed a loving Father. I know that Jesus Christ is our Savior. I know also that Joseph Smith was and is a prophet of God. I know this with all my heart. I know that we have a living prophet leading the Church today, and I love and sustain him as such. And I sustain all the authorities of the Church. I can say with all my heart that I know these things are true and not merely that I believe them. For this knowledge, I will always be grateful. I leave this testimony and witness of the truth in the sacred name of Jesus Christ. Amen.